9780902888074

D1784850

The
CALNE BRANCH

by
G.H.J. Tanner

Research by Brian Lovelock

Photographs by Donald Lovelock

Oxford Publishing Co · Oxford

© Oxford Publishing Co. 1972

SBN 902888 07 2

Printed in the City of Oxford

Published by
Oxford Publishing Co,
5 Lewis Close,
Risinghurst,
Oxford.

FOREWORD

Whilst living with my Grandparents during the first World War, I have a vivid recollection of intriguing references to "the cinder track" and to "Black Dog Siding" and subsequently discovering with some relief that these mysteries were in fact nothing more than the main links for residents within Bowood Park with the big Worlds of Calne and Chippenham outside. Nevertheless, the carefully locked iron gate leading to the cinder track situated close to a cave rejoicing in the strange name of "The Crooked Mustard" and the centre of many childish fantasies, was long an object of considerable awe to me.

It was not until 1950, by which time Mr. Douglas Lovelock had bought the station cottage, outbuildings and some of the yard from me that I travelled on the Calne Branch Line. We were then living at Buckhill and we could set our watches by the friendly rattle of the "Calne Flyer" as it went bustling over the iron bridge. Mr. Lovelock was then our immediate neighbour and an old friend of the family. I congratulate him, his son and his grandson on their part in the production of this interesting publication.

Lansdowne
18. vi. 72.

THE CALNE BRANCH LINE

It is perhaps unique that Mr. Douglas Lovelock, during his period as railwayman in charge at Black Dog Halt, came into ownership of part of the premises on which he worked and indeed received a rent from his employers for storing merchandise on his land.

From the Marquess of Lansdowne, Mr. Lovelock acquired not only the station house, but the loading platform and adjoining land, together with nearby sheds. When sugar beet was dumped on the loading platform to await loading, Mr. Lovelock received a payment from British Rail for the facilities which he was supplying to his former employer.

When the track was taken up and the contractors were given orders to burn down all buildings, Mr. Lovelock was able to get them to agree to him personally taking down the buildings at Black Dog and removing the stonework on the platform.

Today Mr. Lovelock still has woodwork from the buildings and some of the stonework faithfully preserved at his home in Calne.

INTRODUCTION

Today the branch railway line from Chippenham to Calne is but a memory. Part of its course has become a nature trail, an iron bridge which carried the line over the busy London to Bath Road (A4) has been removed, while at Calne a factory manufacturing data processing equipment for the computer industry the world over, occupies well over half of what was formerly the busy goods yard.

Yet for 102 years, until its closure to all traffic on September 18th, 1965, the Chippenham to Calne branch not only linked Wiltshire market towns six miles apart, but it became one of the best known branch railway lines in the country.

There was good reason for this as Calne was the railhead for large Royal Air Force establishments at Compton Bassett and Yatesbury during the Second World War and, in the course of their duties, many thousands of Servicemen and women were conveyed to and from Chippenham by the affectionately termed 'Calne Bunk'.

On an even wider scale attention was focussed on this branch line by specially labelled 'Siphon C' parcel vans which left Calne daily (Saturdays excepted) with the products of the local bacon factory. The vans had special yellow side plates, together with roof boards labelled in striking black letters, *Harris's Wiltshire Sausages*, which gave details of their workings. Calne to Newcastle, Calne—Manchester, Calne—Paddington, Calne—Portsmouth, Calne—Cardiff, to name but a few, could be seen by those who watched the top expresses thunder past in various parts of the country.

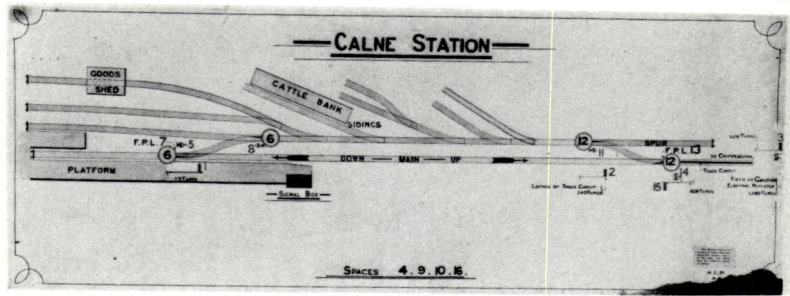

Calne signal box track layout.

THE BEGINNINGS

But first things first. To go back to the beginning one has to cast an eye on what remains of the once-prosperous Calne branch of the Wilts. and Berks. Canal. It was the inability of this section of waterway to cope efficiently enough with the requirements of local industry which brought the railway to Calne.

The Wiltshire bacon-curing industry, founded and operated at Calne by members of the Harris family, had shown a marked advancement with the introduction of ice into the manufacturing process. This had been obvious to Mr. George Harris when he visited America in 1847 to study industrial techniques. However, to bring to Calne by barge such commodities as ice, coal, or salt too for that matter, was a slow and laborious process. Moreover, demand for Wiltshire bacon and other pork products was coming from a rapidly expanding area. A modern transport system was the only answer, and in the 1860s there was nothing more up to date than a railway.

Having said this, it is not surprising to find the names of three members of the Harris family on the board of directors of the Calne Railway Company. Indeed, four members of the Harris family subscribed more than half the capital required for the project.

However, the line which was eventually opened was not the first designed with the object of serving Calne. A project of 1845 by the London, Bristol and South Wales Direct Railway involved the designation of a route which would have taken the line right through the centre of Calne. The route was a straight one from Maidenhead to Chippenham and, had the line been built, it would have run through the northern parts of Calne with a station at the junction of Wood Street and Oxford Road. This would have entailed the demolition of eleven cottages and a blacksmith's shop. Netham Giles, of London, was the architect and the engineer was Francis Giles. But the line was never built.

Instead a special meeting was convened, presided over by the Mayor. Its object was the formation of a company whose task it would be to bring a railway to Calne. In spite of opposition by Mr. James C. Hale, a local wharfinger and coal merchant, who, in his own interests, wanted the canal to Calne kept open as long as possible, a resolution proposed by a Mr. Cowdrey and seconded by Mr. George Harris left in no doubt the popular opinion on the issue. Their resolution was, 'That it is highly desirable and will prove very advantageous to Calne and the neighbourhood to have a line of railway from the town to join the Great Western

Railway at or near Chippenham station.' Mr. Hale could find no support for a counter proposal 'That this meeting does not pledge itself to support the projected railway between Calne and Chippenham.'

He was, in fact, the only person at the meeting to vote against Mr. Cowdrey's resolution. Having taken the initial steps to bring a line of railway to Calne, those concerned lost no time in forming the Calne Railway Company and seeking parliamentary approval for the project. Parliament granted the necessary Act on May 15th, 1860 and this permitted the company to raise capital of £35,000 and up to £11,600 in loans. James Baird Burke was appointed engineer to the project. By comparison with many other lines, the constructional work involved was easy, especially as there were no tunnels required. Early records tell how the Calne Railway Company was fortunate to find an excellent bed of stone on the land owned by Mr. Benjamin Bailey, a Calne corn dealer and miller, who lived at The Highlands in Silver Street (now Vern Leaze). Mr. Bailey operated the old Calne town mill and another mill at Berhills, Calne. The stone was sufficient for the company to build all their bridges (with one exception), and to make all their roads and ballast the entire branch line. During excavations near Stanley Abbey several skeletons and many curious old coins were unearthed.

A report by the engineer to the directors dated September 13th, 1862, states that should the weather continue favourable, and subject to the previous rate of progress being maintained, the whole of the excavations and the greater part of the masonry would be completed in about three months. 'The contractor expects to have the whole of the permanent sleepers and about 350 tons of the permanent rails on the line in the course of the month,' the report adds.

Calne Railway official seal.

THE OPENING

At last the 5 miles 24 chains of rail had been laid and the line was opened to goods traffic only. The first train arrived in Calne at 8.30 a.m. on October 29th, 1863, loaded with 100 pigs and other merchandise, chiefly coal.

The line was built in the broad gauge of 7'0½" between the rails and after a visit by a Board of Trade inspector, who, on making tests, passed the line safe for public traffic, it was announced that the line would be open to passengers on Tuesday, November 3rd, 1863.

An unofficial holiday in Calne marked the opening of the line to passenger traffic. All shops were closed, and members of the 4th Wiltshire Volunteer Corps Band paraded through the streets in uniform. At 10.00 a.m. the bandsmen led 60 employees of Harris's to the railway station where a large number of people awaited the arrival of the excursion train to Bath which was to open the line.

Local historians record how it was raining heavily at the time, and go on to estimate that 1,000 passengers travelled on the train, while many more were left behind through lack of carriage space.

At no time did the Calne Railway Company have its own locomotives. On May 28th, 1862, the company entered into an agreement with the Great Western Railway under which the latter company undertook to run the line for 55 per cent of the gross receipts.

On November 30th, 1865, a plan was published to extend the line a quarter of a mile from Calne station to join up with the North and South Wilts Railway which was to have run past Calne in a North-West—South-East direction. But the plan was never brought into being.

A report of the twenty-second half-yearly meeting of the Calne Railway Company's shareholders, held at Calne Town Hall on Friday, September 29th, 1871, shows that traffic and receipts were substantially greater than those for the relative period of 1870.

Earnings exceeded £12. 10s. per mile per week. Total receipts for the half-year ended June 30th, 1871, amounted to £1,982. 4s. 1d., an excess of £236. 4s. 2d. over the figure for the year ended June 30th, 1870. Other increases were coal and mineral traffic from 2,361 tons to 3,001 tons with receipts increasing from £123. 18s. 3d. to £161. 12s.; general merchandise 3,583 tons (£781. 11s. 2d.) to 4,333 tons (£925. 16s. 1d.) and cattle 13,664 (£171. 2s. 3d.) to 17,052 (£213. 16s. 6d.).

In 1874 the line was converted to the standard 4'8½" gauge we know today, the work being carried out between Friday evening,

August 14th, and the following Monday, during which period no trains ran. The line was vested in the Great Western Railway Company from July 1892.

With traffic at the Calne terminus showing substantial increases annually, the station underwent extensive renovations and enlargement in 1895.

Early pictures show an engine shed to the north of the passenger platform. This occupied an area between the water tank and the signal box, the land, in the days before the closure, forming the allotments of the two signalmen who manned the box at Calne.

At the outset there were no intermediate stations on the line, but later a halt was built at Stanley Bridge, and the Marquess of Lansdowne's private station at Black Dog was also constructed. The latter was named after a stretch of the old London to Bath coach road which passed nearby, while Stanley Bridge owes its name to a 13th century abbey which stood close at hand, but has now completely disappeared. Some of the abbey's stonework has, however, been incorporated into the modern Calne Roman Catholic Church of St. Edmund Rich.

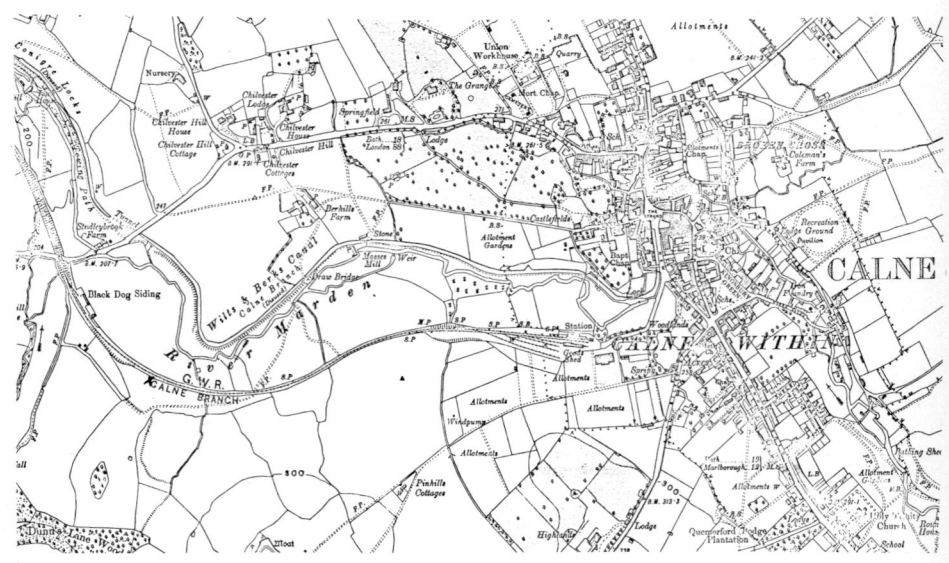

Map of Calne Branch at the Calne Terminus.

THE LINE

From Chippenham the Calne branch trains followed the main line towards London for a short distance, past the now demolished Chippenham East signal box, before curving off in a south-easterly direction. At the approach to the point where the track became single, a notice stood which stated that no engine classified blue or red was allowed on the branch. This was very close to the Chippenham engine shed (a sub-shed of Swindon), which now no longer exists, but where much of the motive power used on the branch was based.

From the Great Western Railway main line, the Calne branch entered a cutting which ended close to a single span iron bridge, named the Black Bridge (originally a wooden structure). This was so named on account of its colouring and carried the line over the River Avon.

From the bridge, was traversed flat country, much of which was rich farmland, until Stanley Bridge Halt was reached. This was two miles from Chippenham. The platform was on the west side and the shelter was of the pagoda type much favoured by the G.W.R. There was once a wooden-type building on the platform, which was provided to house milk churns, but some years before the line closed the old milk shed was demolished.

In the fields by the over-bridge, which carried a minor road to Chippenham, could be seen Great Western boundary posts of 1885, 1889, and 1900.

Perhaps the most picturesque section of the line was that between Stanley Bridge Halt and Black Dog Halt. From Stanley Bridge the railway ascended a gradient of 1 in 80, passing the Roman village of Studley high on a hill to the south and crossing the old Wilts. and Berks. canal. The crossing was originally made by a bridge, but later, when the waterway fell into complete disuse, its course was filled in, the bridge dispensed with and the track lowered.

Still following a course close to the River Marden, which first came to the rail traveller's notice near Stanley, the line (which was carried by steel sleepers for a considerable distance) wended its way through woodland at Hazeland, where nightingales can still be heard. It then emerged and crossed the A4 road at Black Dog by an iron bridge.

Like Stanley Bridge, the platform and buildings at Black Dog were on the west side of the line. Black Dog, a station with a unique history which will be recounted later, had a carriage approach, a goods platform and a single siding, together with a ground frame containing the levers necessary for operating the points. A house was provided for the

Stationmaster. Black Dog was 4¼ miles from Chippenham and from there the line curved eastwards to Calne.

A fixed distant signal, now preserved in the garden of the Calne home of Mr. Donald Lovelock, stood on the Calne side of Black Dog station and having passed it the crews of trains approaching from Chippenham had one other home main line signal to observe before reaching the platform at Calne. This signal also incorporated a smaller arm used to control entry into the goods yard.

In the opposite direction there was a starter signal on the platform at Calne, an advanced starter beyond the signal box and an outer home signal some 500 yards further down the line.

A fixed distant signal was positioned on the Calne side of the Black Bridge, and near the Cocklebury over-bridge on the outskirts of Chippenham there was an outer home signal.

Home and distant signals were used to control entry to the down main line at Chippenham, the end of the branch.

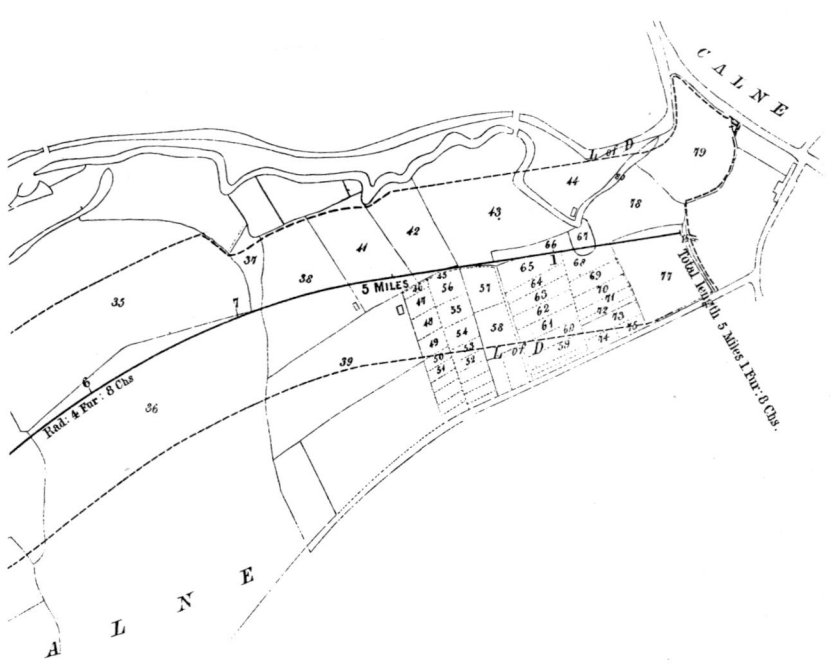

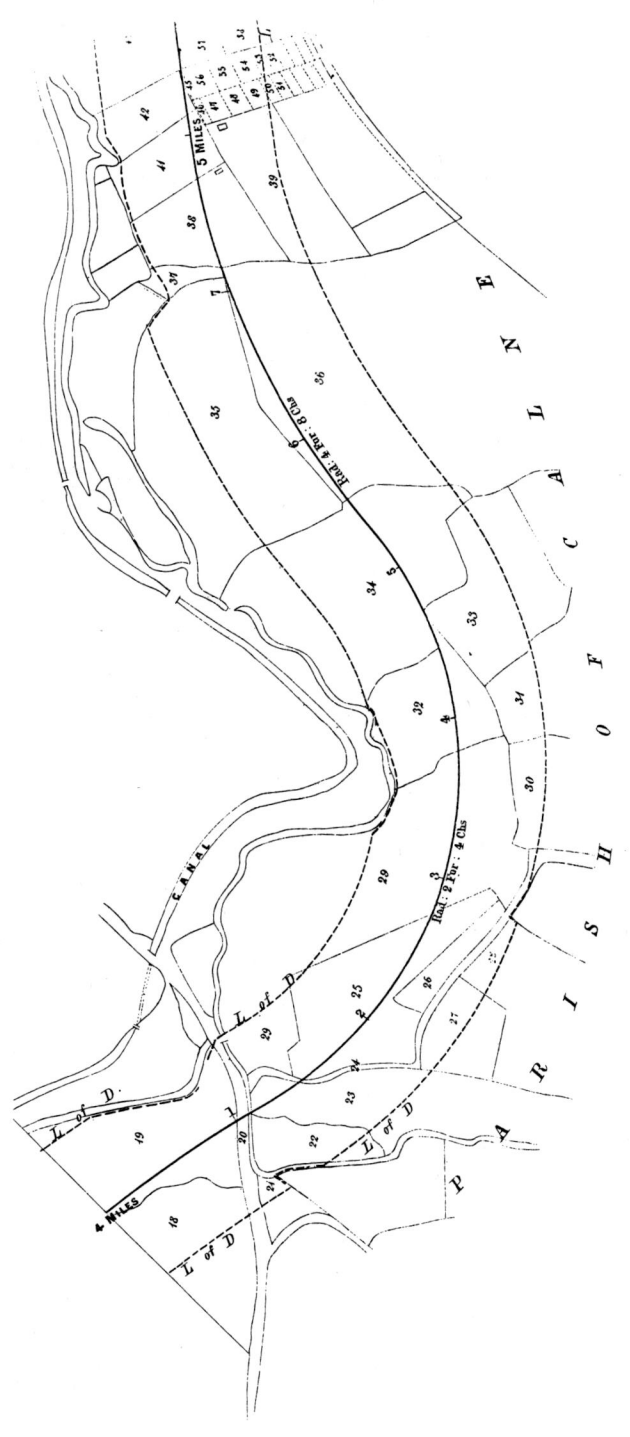

11

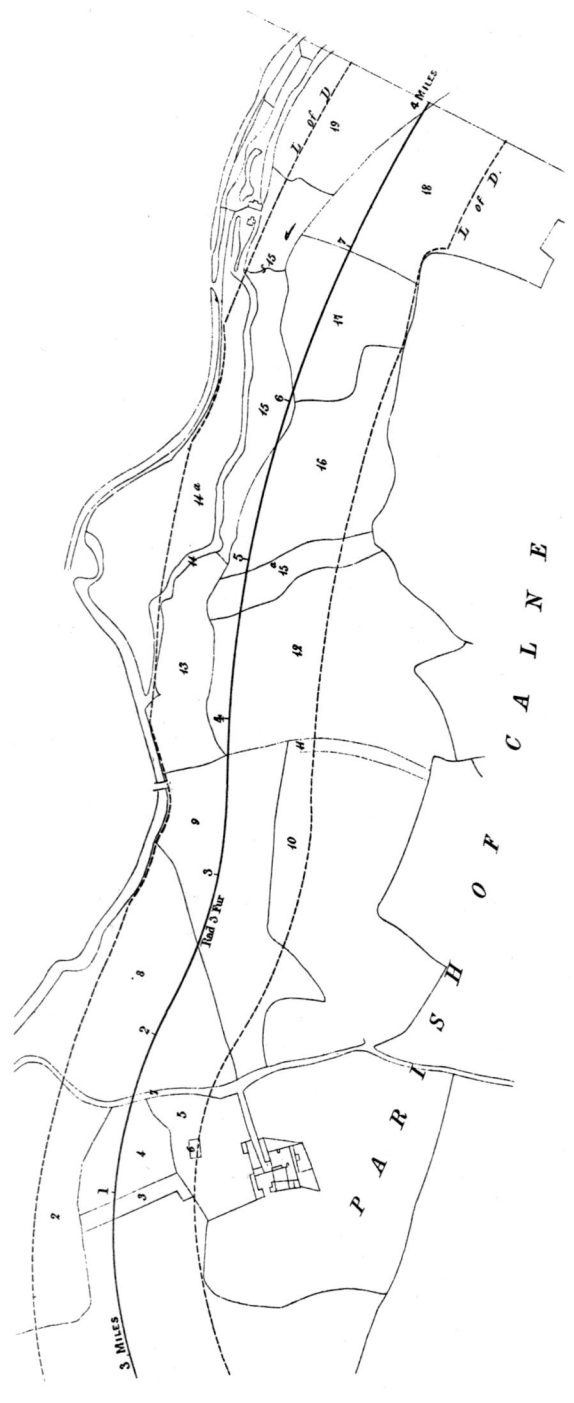

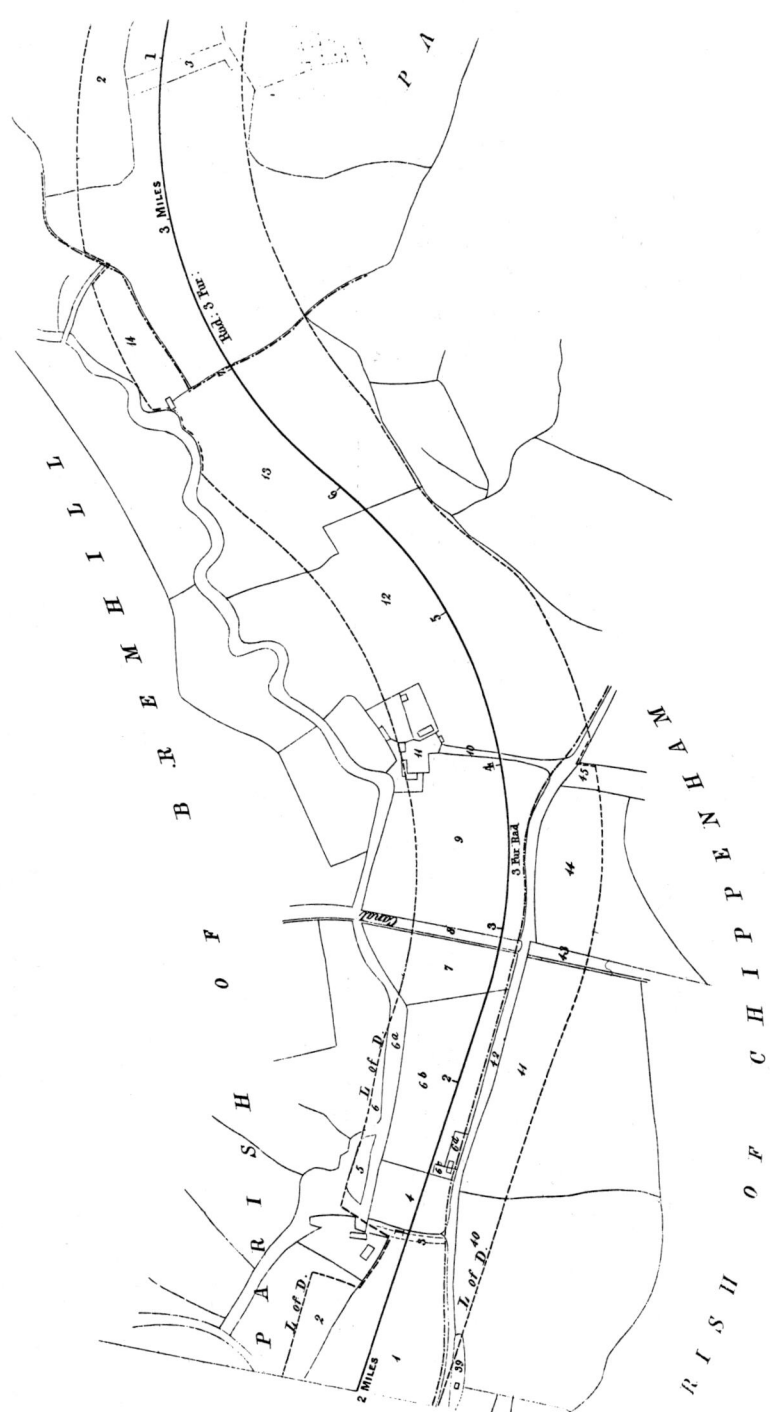

13

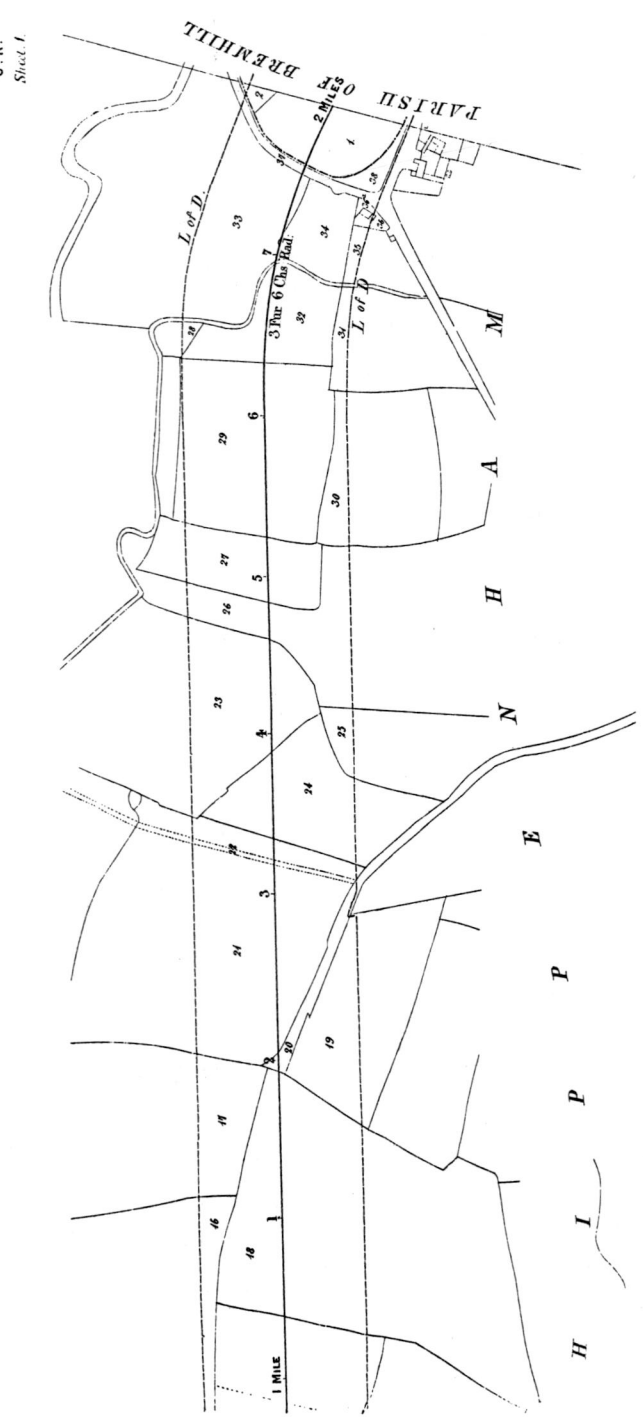

14

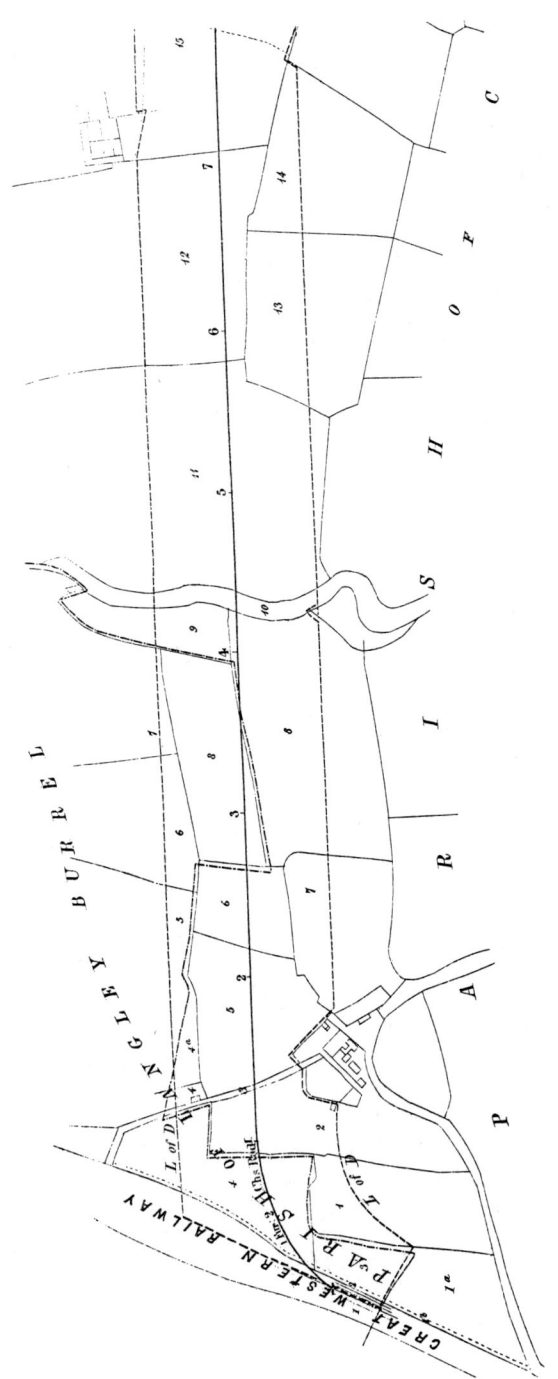

15

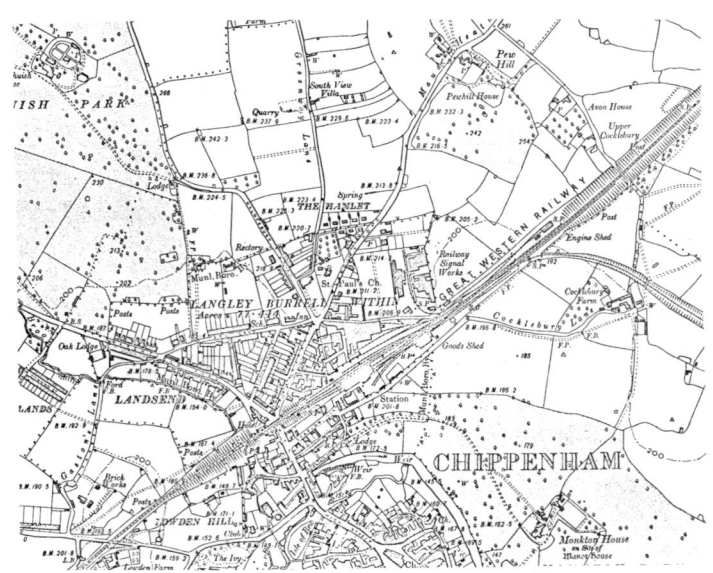

Map of Calne Branch at the Chippenham Terminus.

Stanley Bridge Halt looking towards Calne

Dotted line showing route of proposed North and South Wiltshire Railway.

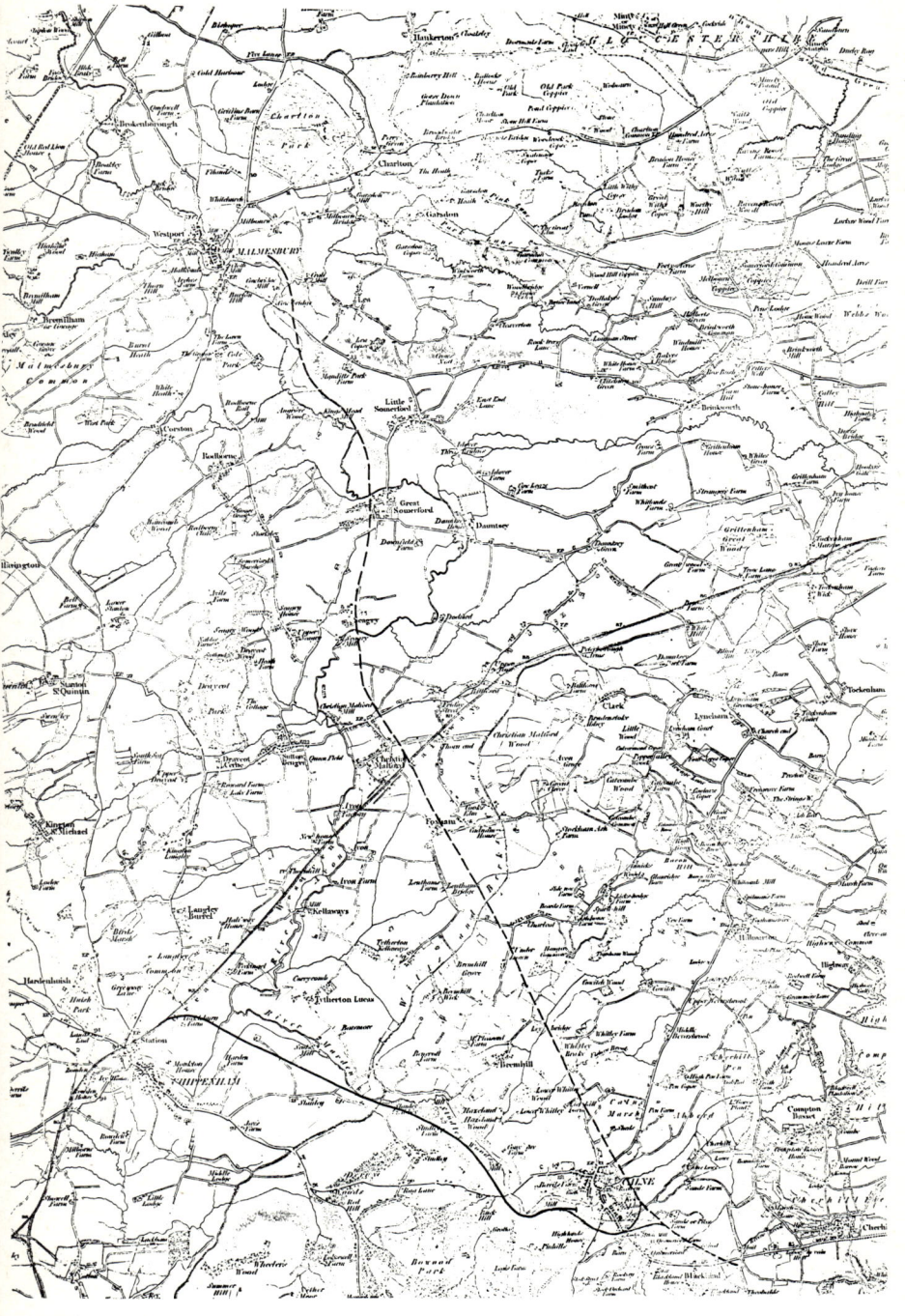

Plan dated November 30th, 1865 to extend the Calne branch a quarter of a mile from Calne station to join up with the North and South Wiltshire railway. This line was authorised by Parliament in 1866 and was to have run past Calne in a North-West—South-East direction.

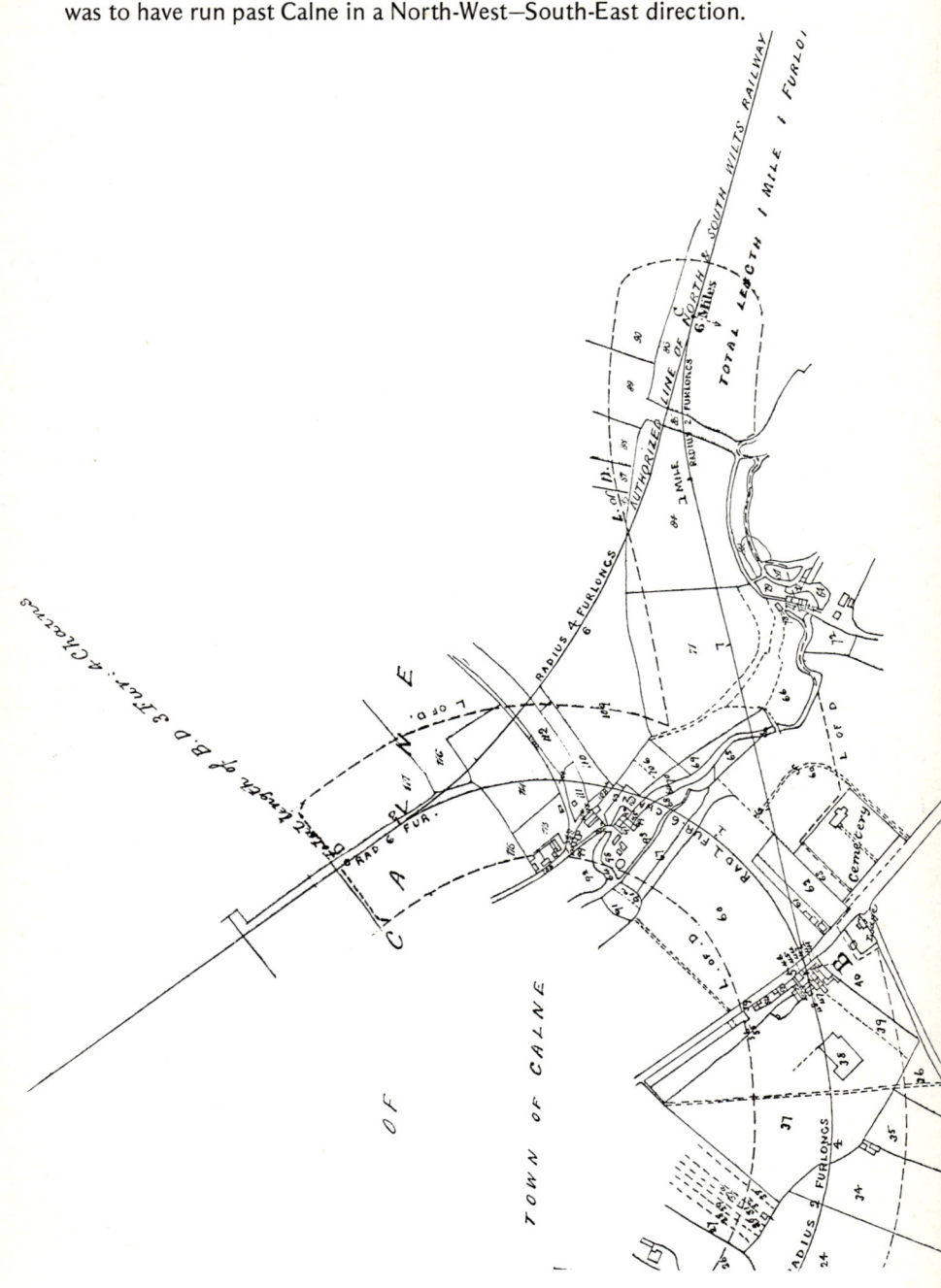

LIST OF GRADIENT BOARDS ON THE CALNE BRANCH

Miles	Chains	
0	52	Rising 100 to Chippenham. Level to Calne.
0	64	Rising 100 to Calne. Level to Chippenham.
1	2	Falling 100 to Chippenham. Falling 220 to Calne.
1	25	Rising 220 to Chippenham. Falling 154 to Calne.
1	45	Rising 154 to Chippenham. Level to Calne.
1	62	Level to Chippenham. Falling 139 to Calne.
2	½	Rising 139 to Chippenham. Rising 80 to Calne.
2	38½	Falling 80 to Chippenham. Level to Calne.
3	20	Falling 100 to Chippenham. Rising 366 to Calne.
3	48	Falling 366 to Chippenham. Rising 133 to Calne.
3	59	Falling 133 to Chippenham. Rising 100 to Calne.
3	79	Falling 100 to Chippenham. Rising 100 to Calne.
4	10¾	Level to Chippenham. Rising 100 to Calne.
4	35¾	Falling 100 to Chippenham. Rising 96 to Calne.
4	62	Falling 96 to Chippenham. Level to Calne.
4	74	Level to Chippenham. Rising 100 to Calne.
5	4	Falling 100 to Chippenham. Rising 90 to Calne.

Chippenham Shed scene.

CALNE STATION

The station at Calne had its platform on the north side. During the 1914-18 war new sidings and a loading platform were added. In 1942 the passenger platform was extended as far as the signal box so that eight coach trains could be accommodated. The cost of this extension was initially met by H.M. Government, the railway company paying for it after the war so that the facility could be retained. At the same time a corrugated iron structure was built for the storage of incoming parcels and the porters' trolleys. This was sited between the porters' messroom and the end of the line, facing the approach road. A wooden booking office and waiting room (now in the ownership of Mr. John Croker, of Cherhill near Calne, a one-time Calne booking clerk) was added between the main station buildings and the disused water tank.

A wooden canopy was set in place at the rear of the station buildings to provide protection for travellers who arrived at the station in horse-drawn coaches. This started its life as a part of the goods shed. Immediately opposite the passenger platform was a milk dock with access to the road, to facilitate easy loading. At the end of this platform stood a loading gauge, while behind this was the stone built goods shed. A loading platform equipped with wooden pens for the accommodation of animals ran for much of the length of the goods yard, at the west end of which was a hand operated light crane. The private siding of C. & T. Harris (Calne) Ltd., built in 1927-28, began at the rear of the goods shed and ran alongside Harris's own loading platform where goods traffic only was dealt with. At one time up to twenty loaded trucks were despatched on normal working days.

The siding then gave access to Harris's own private goods yard where the company's coal and salt wagons were stabled. The yard terminated under a high wall, on the opposite side of which is Spring Lane. The rails there, some of which still remain, were the closest ever laid to the Calne town centre. A large wooden gate was provided to mark the division of the boundaries of the Great Western Railway Company and C. & T. Harris (Calne) Ltd. There were also gates in the station approach road which were often closed and locked when the station was not in use. A large goods office stood just inside these gates close to the sidings, and on the boundary of Harris's private land. Outside was a weighbridge of 20 tons capacity. When the wooden booking office and waiting room was opened in 1942 the parcels clerical staff moved into what had been the booking office, and the adjoining general waiting room became the Stationmaster's office.

The station was lit by gas until the final years of its working life when electricity was installed.

The Calne station buildings and goods yard stood on 4¼ acres of land purchased from the Marquess of Lansdowne at a cost of £425. Calne signal box had sixteen levers and the line was worked on the electric token system.

In October 1904 the Great Western Railway Company started running a bus service between Calne and Marlborough, and buses called at Calne station. The service was later taken over by the Bristol Omnibus Company.

Calne Station late 1800s. Engine shed showing just behind water tank.

Calne Station looking towards Chippenham.

Calne Station.

Photo by Wiltshire Newspapers

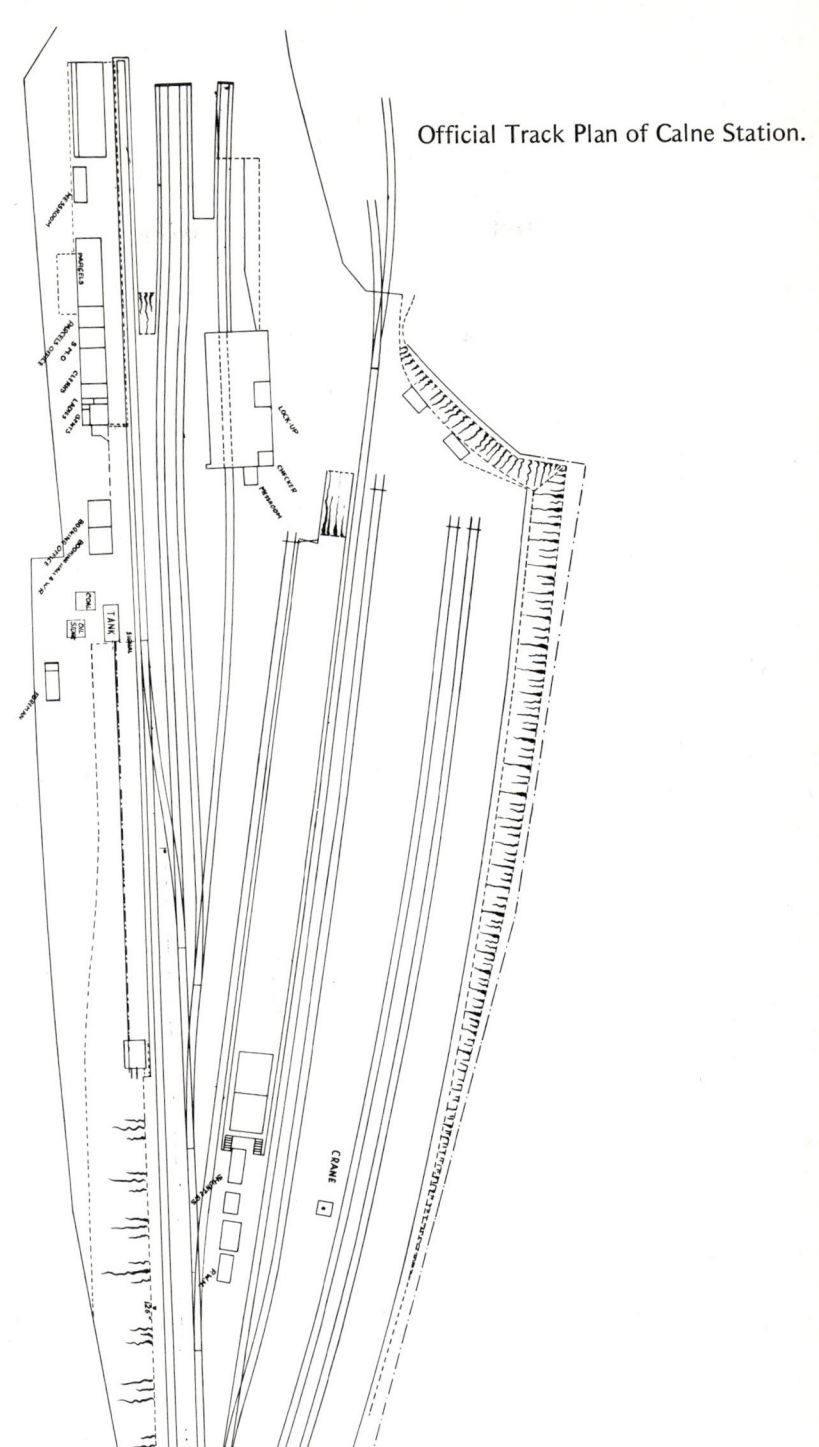

Official Track Plan of Calne Station.

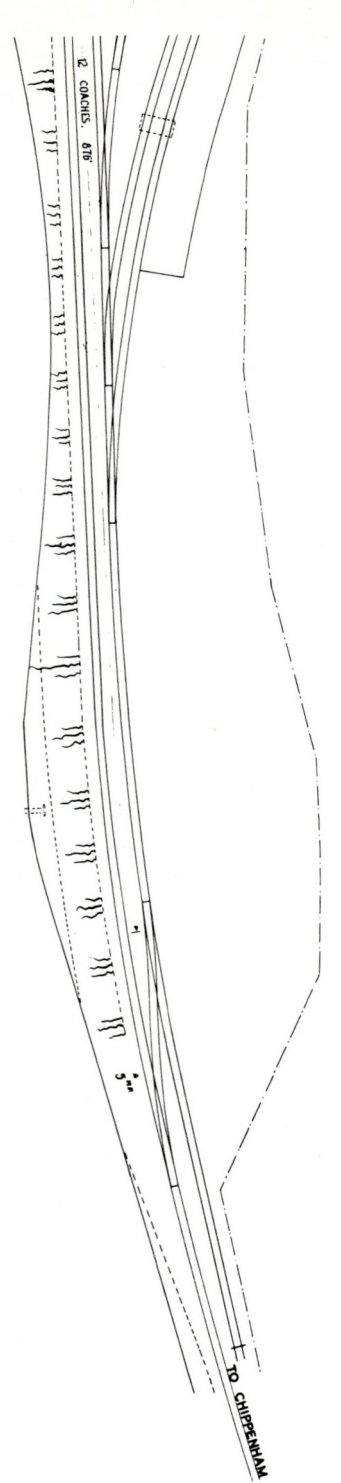

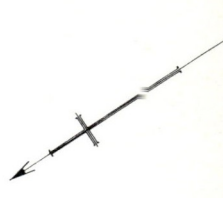

12 COACHES. 876'

3 m.p.

TO CHIPPENHAM.

24

Calne Station and Goods Yard. Photograph taken about 1906

Photograph taken about 1910.

Calne Station. Photograph taken about 1910. Note Steam Rail Car.

BLACK DOG

Much more interesting, however, is the history of Black Dog station which, from its construction in 1874 until September 15th, 1952, never appeared in any public timetable. During this time it served as the private station of the Marquess of Lansdowne and until 1930 boasted a fully fledged Stationmaster.

Early records show that Black Dog station had a signal box in its own right. There were also four signals, two on either side of the station. The signal box and the platform were the only buildings erected by the Great Western Railway, the shelter being set in place during the winter of 1876-77 by the Marquess of Lansdowne.

However, Lord Lansdowne had no objection to members of the general public alighting from or boarding trains there. When the Calne Railway Company was formed, Lord Lansdowne secured a quarter of an acre of land at Black Dog, near the turnpike road as it was called in those days. This enabled coal and other heavy goods for his private use to be unloaded at the nearest point to his mansion at Bowood.

At this time the railway company had plans to construct an adjoining yard at Black Dog and, by using the same access from Turn Pike Road to provide facilities for nearby flour mills and the supply of coal to the Derry Hill and Studley area.

However, due to financial difficulties, this idea never materialised, but in later years the siding was used by a coal merchant and a small weighbridge was built and brought into use. Eventually, after lengthy negotiations, the directors of the Calne Railway Company on May 26th, 1871 agreed that the Great Western Railway Company should construct the siding, but this was not completed until April 1875. Before this the Great Western Railway Company had built a platform at Black Dog some 80'6" in length with 18' slopes at each end. In the winter of 1876-77 Lord Lansdowne had erected on the platform a shed which cost him £55. 16s. 4d. The accounts contained such entries as 6,800 bricks £8. 10s., 800 slates £10. 4s., three lamps (oil) £4. 4s. and a total wage bill of £7. 12s. The understanding was that his Lordship had a right to move the shed at any time, but it remained unmoved until the line was closed.

Other estimates in respect of Black Dog show a figure of £290 for the construction of the siding, and £150 for the provision of a road and a bridge over a stream. Lord Lansdowne contributed £30 towards the latter expenditure, and he also paid the Great Western Railway Company 8s. per week towards the wages of the Stationmaster, in addition

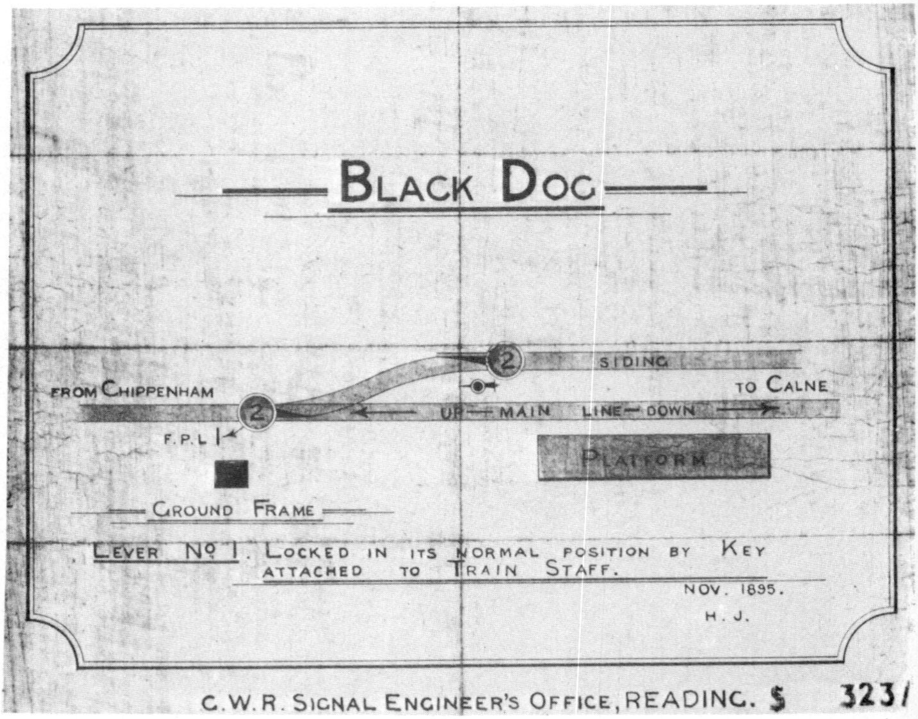

BLACK DOG

FROM CHIPPENHAM

SIDING

TO CALNE

UP — MAIN LINE — DOWN

F.P.L

Platform

GROUND FRAME

LEVER Nº 1. LOCKED IN ITS NORMAL POSITION BY KEY ATTACHED TO TRAIN STAFF.

NOV. 1895.

H. J.

G.W.R. SIGNAL ENGINEER'S OFFICE, READING. 323/

Black Dog Halt looking towards Calne. About 1960.

Black Dog Halt.

Black Dog taken from bridge over A4 trunk road. Early 1950s.

to providing him with four tons of coal a year and a rent-free house.

As early as April 1898, the Great Western Railway Company was requesting Lord Lansdowne to allow a board with the words BLACK DOG STATION to be set in place on the platform. But his Lordship's permission was not forthcoming and more than fifty years were to elapse before a nameboard was displayed at the station. To the siding at Black Dog came a wide variety of commodities for the Lansdowne household. Loaded there, on occasions, were valuables which Lord Lansdowne required temporarily transferring to his London residence. The first Stationmaster, Mr. George Neate, moved into a house situated close to the railway line. This was originally constructed for occupation by the estate foreman, although no holder of that position ever lived there.

In Mr. Neate's day traffic flourished. A cinder path connected the estate to the station, this being a quarter of a mile in length. It was kept in immaculate condition by the estate staff who spent at least one day a week on this task.

With Black Dog not appearing in any public timetable, passengers from Calne had to book to Chippenham, and later to Stanley Bridge Halt. Those travelling in the opposite direction had to take tickets to Calne. All merchandise conveyed from Calne was charged at rates applicable to Chippenham, while traffic from Chippenham was charged at Calne rates.

In June 1911 Mr. William Cockram succeeded the previous stationmaster. Prior to taking up this appointment he was employed as a parcel porter at Chippenham. During his stay Mr. Cockram had a military unit stationed in outbuildings opposite the station. This was during the 1914-18 war when a top level Cabinet meeting took place in a coach berthed in the siding.

Mr. Cockram, who left in 1930 to take charge of Congresbury station in Somerset, did however have the distinction of being the last Stationmaster at Black Dog for, on the appointment of Mr. Douglas Lovelock, the post was reduced to that of Grade 1 Porter. Mr. Lovelock, who came from Axbridge, Somerset, was surprised when asked to attend an interview for the post as he had not even applied for it. His surprise was even greater when the rules and regulations associated with the job were read to him. They laid down firmly that he must advance no political views when dealing with nobility, and that he must endeavour to keep clear of the local court where Lord Lansdowne was chairman of the magistrates.

On moving to Black Dog, Mr. Lovelock found the changing times had been responsible for the withdrawal of several privileges enjoyed by former Stationmasters. The station house was now let to him for a nominal rent and no free coal was provided.

In 1950 the station house, which bears the Lansdowne crest on an outer wall, was offered for sale, together with several outbuildings and part of the station yard. It was then that Mr. Lovelock stepped in with a firm bid which secured him part of the premises on which he worked. Later, he in turn disposed of the outbuildings to Mr. Reg Wilkins, who converted them into a modern bungalow.

With the publication of the British Railways (Western Region) time-table of September 15th, 1952, the station appeared in a public time-table for the first time. The occasion was marked by the longest foot-note in the timetable which gave details of how trains would stop if the appropriate signal was given by people wishing to board them. At this time a nameplate was set in place on the platform.

On February 1st, 1960 Black Dog became an unstaffed halt, al-though the siding could still be used on advance notice being given to the Stationmaster at Calne. A local coalmerchant was the last regular user of the siding, and the end came on November 1st, 1963, when the rails were lifted. Two days later the points were taken out. So, too, were the controlling levers housed in a ground frame. But the station buildings remained until the branch line was lifted in 1967.

Dummy Signal on catch points at Black Dog.

THE WORKINGS

In December 1863 five passenger trains were run in each direction every weekday on the line. Also scheduled were regular freight trains.

The introduction of steam railcars in 1905 (in connection with which Stanley Bridge Halt was opened on April 3rd that year) brought with it not only an increase in the passenger service, but also the introduction of special first class compartments for the use of Lord Lansdowne. One of these, which retired Calne railwaymen remember clearly, was Trailer 13. If the train was full and Lord Lansdowne was not among its passengers, the special compartment could be used by the general public. The steam railcars could travel equally well in either direction, and a cab was provided at each end for the driver.

On occasions more than one trailer formed a train, and besides operating between Chippenham and Calne the railcars also made daily trips between Calne and Bath. These railcars were the forerunners of the multiple unit diesels which were introduced on the line in September 1958. However, from the mid-1930s, when the last steam railcars were withdrawn from service, the passenger trains were worked by the 0–4–2T locomotives of the 4800 (later 1400) class and the 0–6–0T of the 5400 class, all of which were specially equipped with the auto gear necessary for push-pull workings with trailers. If engines not equipped with auto-gear were used on passenger trains into Calne, then the locomotives had to perform a running round operation so that they headed the coaches on the return to Chippenham. It is of interest to record, how, until the end of the Second World War, some of the 'trailers' used on the line were wooden-sided and lit by gas. They had, in fact, started their lives as steam railcars in the early 1900s.

During the period between the steam railcars and the diesels, first class compartments were removed from these trailers. The only trains to provide regular first class accommodation was one which left Calne at 10.50 a.m. and another at 2.42 p.m. They originated at Bristol and were usually in the charge of a 4500 class 2–6–2T locomotive from the Bristol (Bath Road) shed. Westbury (Wilts.) based engines also worked some of the passenger trains to and from Calne. Goods trains were mainly in the charge of 0–6–0T engines, some of them of the open cab variety and built prior to 1900.

In the days before the 1914-18 war, a milk train left Calne every weekday. Also handled daily at the station was a truck of fish for the local merchants. It was in the years of the 1939-45 war, however, that the pattern of locomotives used on the branch line fell by the wayside.

Photograph taken from Hazeland Road Bridge.

3604 on the 1.12 pm Saturdays only Calne/Weston-S-Mare
8783 on freight in Siding

Photograph taken from Hazeland Road bridge

Calne Yard early 1960s.

From that time, until the steam workings were ended, Ivatt L.M.R. Class 2 2–6–0s, Ivatt L.M.R. Class 2 2–6–2T, Standard Class 3 2–6–2T, 2251 Class 0–6–0s and even 0–6–0Ts of the 9400 class, though not officially permitted, were observed working trains on the branch.

Initially it was the building of No. 2 R.A.F. Radio School at Yatesbury with accommodation for 10,000 airmen and airwomen which brought additional freight traffic to Calne in the form of building equipment and the sectional wooden huts which provided both living and classroom accommodation on this camp.

Then, when R.A.F. Yatesbury was complete, work on No. 3 R.A.F. Radio School at Compton Bassett was started and once more Calne was the railhead.

So, within the space of a few years, the branch line from Chippenham to Calne was called on to meet the comings and goings of some 20,000 Service personnel, their personal baggage and the equipment used to train them.

This was in addition to the incoming pigs for C. & T. Harris Ltd., the arrival of which was signified by a special blast on the whistle of the station shunting engine, so that drovers could lose no time in coming from the factory to the station where the livestock were speedily off-loaded and driven through the town's streets to the factory slaughterhouse. The wagons which brought the pigs to Calne were then cleaned, whitewashed and made ready for returning empty. When there was no convenient goods service, the pigs came in by passenger train, providing they were being conveyed in 'XP' wagons.

During this time the local coal traffic continued to flourish. Also during the 1939-45 war, fuel used to fire the boilers at the R.A.F. Stations came into Calne by rail. Harris's incoming loads of coal and salt continued, while the Calne terminus was also called on to cope with ever-increasing traffic in the form of animal feeds and grain for local millers.

The outgoing freight traffic included cattle from the local market and through truckloads of non-perishable commodities from Harris's factory. To take charge of this the 0–6–0Ts were supplemented by the Dean standard goods 0–6–0s of the 2301 class. They worked tender-first into Calne for shunting purposes and were not popular with the crews on account of the poor protection from the weather which their cabs afforded. Engines of the 4500 class 2–6–2T were also regularly used on the freight services.

For some years during this period there were three scheduled freight workings in and out of Calne on weekdays. They left Chippenham at 5.55 a.m., 11.10 a.m. and 2.35 p.m., returning at 9.40 a.m., 1.25 p.m. and 5.55 p.m., after the locomotives had carried out shunting duties in the Calne goods yard. If the first freight service was not required to convey wagons, the practice was for the locomotive to return to Chippenham with the 9 a.m. passenger service, giving the unusual sight of a single trailer with a locomotive at each end.

The 5.55 p.m. freight train often left Calne with up to fifty empty wagons behind the engine, although the maximum number officially permitted was 35 from Chippenham to Calne, and 40 in the opposite direction. Mr. Jack Kington, who spent much of his railway career as a signalman at Calne, remembers how, on Christmas Day 1939, a special goods train left Calne with no less than 86 empty wagons behind the engine. The yard was shunted and the train made up in the early hours of that Christmas Day and the wagons to be attached were stabled in three sidings. The engine hauling the train was driven by Mr. Charlie Gibbons, of Chippenham, and the guard, also from Chippenham, was Mr. Bill Read. When the train left Calne, Mr. Kington had to ask the signalman on duty at Chippenham East Box to give it a clear run on to the main line. Had the signals been at danger on that part of the branch line close to the main line at Chippenham, the locomotive would not have been able to re-start the train on the 1 in 33 gradient. This special Christmas morning train of empties, which ran through to Box to be put in the sidings, was necessary to relieve acute congestion in the Calne goods yard. At this time goods traffic bound for Calne was being held back as far away as Didcot and Oxford because the sidings were full, and as soon as a train of empty wagons reached Chippenham, another train left the junction with loaded wagons to fill the vacant siding space. The 8.5 a.m. service from Chippenham on weekdays was a mixed one, usually comprising a non-corridor brake third, empty Siphon C vans for Harris's sausages, trucks of pigs and, in fact, anything at Chippenham labelled for Calne which was loaded in an 'XP' van.

In latter years when the 8.5 a.m. from Chippenham became a passenger-only service, it worked back as the 8.25 a.m. from Calne to Bristol which travelled via the unusual route of Chippenham, Melksham, Bradford Junction, Bradford-on-Avon and Bathampton. The 7.25 a.m. passenger train from Calne on school days worked through to Box.

During the Second World War the first passenger train left Chippenham at 6.15 a.m., arriving at Calne at 6.30 a.m. and departing at

2–6–0 Ivatt. 46525 2.20 pm Calne/Chippenham

1400 standing in Calne station

0–6–0 on the 2.53 pm Saturdays only Chippenham/Calne running into Black Dog from Chippenham

0–4–2 1446 on the 11.57 Chippenham/Calne pulling away from Black Dog 19.4.54.

6.35 a.m. for the return trip. In pre-war days the last Calne departure, apart from a late train on Wednesdays and Saturdays, was 9 p.m., but the war changed all of that and an additional departure from Chippenham at 9.40 p.m. on weekdays was instituted. The return service left Calne at 10.5 p.m. The 10.50 p.m. train from Chippenham, which left Calne at 11.10 p.m., continued to run on Wednesdays and Saturdays.

On weekdays, during the peak wartime traffic period, fourteen passenger trains ran in each direction every weekday, with one additional train on Wednesdays and two on Saturdays. The 1.12 p.m. from Calne on Saturdays formed the first part of the 1 p.m. Swindon to Weston-Super-Mare passenger service. It departed Chippenham at 1.25 p.m. and, apart from calls at Corsham and Bath, ran non-stop to Temple Meads, Bristol, and thence on to Weston-Super-Mare. A Swindon engine always worked this train which was formed by eight or more conventional type coaches (very often all corridor stock). Swindon often marked the working by supplying a locomotive which had just come out of workshops having undergone a major overhaul, and which presented an impressive spectacle as it stood sparkling in the platform at Calne awaiting the right of way. The locomotive used was seldom of the same type two weeks running. Consequently, this was a train which local rail enthusiasts would not miss seeing if they could help it.

In the early part of the war, before the passenger platform was lengthened, this train departed from the cattle dock in the goods yard. During the war the single trailers which formed many of the passenger trains on the branch became too small to meet traffic requirements, and so additional trailers were brought into service, and most trains became twin car units.

The 6.35 p.m. passenger train from Chippenham on weekdays was formed by whatever stock chanced to be available there and often comprised an old gas light trailer (once a steam railcar), and a non corridor third. On one dark wartime winter Saturday night there was a minor panic at Calne when this train arrived minus a guard. It was then ascertained that he and about thirty passengers had been left behind as the second coach had not been coupled up at Chippenham. On another occasion a Westbury 5400 0—6—0T arrived on the 4.30 p.m. train from Chippenham short of water. The Calne station staff formed a human chain using every fire bucket on the station to partially replenish the locomotive's water supply. Some passengers helped too, and the driver left under instruction to cut out the scheduled stops at Black Dog and Stanley Bridge if he felt he would not make Chippenham before the water ran out. But he did and another crisis was averted.

The Sunday service at this time comprised seven passenger trains in each direction. There was an additional train which left Calne at 7.45 a.m., but which was never listed in any public timetable. The train, which was formed by a single trailer, came to Calne to shunt the parcels vans on to the main line ready for the morning's loading, and was much used by passengers, chiefly workers and Service personnel, particularly on the return journey to Chippenham. For some years during the war the 8.33 p.m. Sunday passenger train from Bristol worked through to Calne. It was usually one of seven or eight coaches hauled by a 4500 2–6–2T. Often, if sufficient pigs had arrived at Chippenham, a special goods train would be run to Calne on a Sunday morning. The 2,000 specially scheduled parcels vans taking Harris's sausages and other perishable products to all parts of the country continued to run annually. The Chippenham carriage cleaner made daily trips to Calne to wash the nameboards and a special gas cylinder wagon was kept at the station to replenish empty gas tanks on the parcels vans. The first parcels van departure from Calne was by the 2.35 p.m. (formerly 2.42 p.m.) passenger service. Other vans left at 5 p.m. and 5.35 p.m. and the rest at 7.5 p.m.

An additional source of revenue came in the form of horse boxes (Pacos) which took local Shire stallions from a stud farm at Yatesbury on their tours of the land. Stores traffic to and from the R.A.F. base at Lyneham also found its way in and out of Calne in the latter years of the war and after. Hundreds of special troop trains ran in and out of Calne station during the war years when the staff there numbered more than forty. This was a very large staff for a single Branch which shows how busy and important this station was. These troop trains were made up of ten or more coaches and were hauled by either a pair of 4500s 2–6–2Ts or 5700s 0–6–0Ts. A standard Dean goods of the 2301 class headed by a 4500 class was not an uncommon sight on a special troop train out of Calne. The trains usually left from the goods yard having loaded their human cargoes from the cattle bank (the name given to the loading platform). This gave more space than the main passenger platform where four or five parcel vans were berthed. These were there from 9 a.m. until the evening on Mondays to Fridays.

Over the years only one named engine can be clearly recollected as having hauled a train in and out of Calne. This was No. 3443 *Chaffinch*, a 4–4–0 of the 3300 'Bulldog' class which in the early 1940s hauled a special train of R.A.F. personnel bound for Paddington. But, like many of the other locomotives on special troop trains out of Calne, *Chaffinch* gave way at the head on reaching Chippenham to an engine of the 4900

2203 standing at Black Dog on an Engineering train.

5700 Class. The 2.50 p.m. on Calne/Chippenham freight running
through Black Dog. Early 1950s.

'Hall' class. During the locomen's strike in the 1920s, members of the Calne station staff recall that a locomotive of the 3900 'County' class worked into Calne with N.U.R. men on the footplate. This was 3829 *County of Merioneth*. Engines of the 2200 0–6–0 class sometimes came to Calne and in 1955 a standard Class 3 2–6–2T was noted on the branch. Other unusual workings often came when the weed killing train made its annual trip to Calne, while not long before the line was closed heavy snow resulted in a D7000 being entrusted to push a snow-plough from Chippenham. On another occasion when a snowfall disrupted the normal workings, the first passenger train of the day reached Calne at 8.30 a.m. formed by two parcel vans in which passengers had standing accommodation only. There were no complaints from them, however, as the A4 road between Chippenham and Calne was impassable. The train had the effect of restoring communication to Calne which had been cut off from the outside world by deep snowdrifts for several hours previously.

Photograph taken about 1927. Loading C & T Harris parcels in Calne passenger platform.

This train was one of a few to work over the branch during the ASLEF strike of 1955. The driver retired at the end of the week. 30.5.55.

During the period of heavy traffic in the 1939-45 war, the stationmaster at Calne was Mr. Seymour John Harding, who was previously stationmaster at Ludgershall. Black Dog also came under his jurisdiction, while the Chippenham stationmaster was responsible for Stanley Bridge Halt. The chief parcels clerk was Mr. Percy Charles Gleed, who, after the death of Mr. Harding, became stationmaster. Mr. Bertie Reynolds was chief goods clerk and the station foreman was Mr. Horace Poole. The two signalmen both held civic positions in the town. Mr. John Kington was a Justice of the Peace and Mr. Arthur Iles had a spell as a member of Calne Town Council.

During this period the Chippenham drivers who worked the passenger services included Ernie Collett, Ebenezer Ash, Fred Cummings and Tommy Astle. The guards included Arthur Woolley, Jack Bidder, Jack Trout and Percy Vines. Chippenham based porter-guards who came to Calne were Harry Willis and Tommy Neate. On the freight side, brothers Arthur and Bill Read were driver and guard on one of the workings. The permanent way gang, under Mr. George Pound, won several awards for the best kept section of track in the Bristol division.

The branch line was always subjected to a 30 m.p.h. speed limit, but very often the passenger trains were in Calne long before the scheduled fifteen minutes for the trip from Chippenham had elapsed. The unofficial record for the journey was that of Ernie Burrows, of Bath, who, while in charge of a 4500 2—6—2T, cleared Chippenham East Box in 7½ minutes. This was before the 1939-45 war and was on the 10.50 a.m. service out of Calne. Bert Taylor, of the Westbury shed, was another fast mover. At the controls of a 5400 0—6—0T he brought the 12.54 p.m. passenger train from Chippenham into Calne in eight minutes flat. Ebenezer Ash, of Chippenham, could complete the trip in nine minutes in either a 5400 or a 4800 class engine.

Days on the Calne branch during the years before the Second World War did not pass without there being many humorous moments. On a Saturday afternoon, for example, when the station was quiet after its lunchtime outward surge of passenger traffic, the new lad porter was always, on his first or second week of duty, sent to the goods yard to the shunting engine with a request to the driver that the bucket he carried be filled with steam for bringing back to the duty parcel porter. Surprisingly enough, the unsuspecting lad porters always fell for this hoax. Another Saturday afternoon trick gave the Calne leading parcel porter no peace during the time he spent as temporary railwayman in charge of Black Dog Halt. The ancient internal telephone would not stop ringing even when the earpiece was removed. The mouthpiece was a fixture, so all it needed to ensure an afternoon long ring-a-ding-ding at Black Dog was the handle of the Calne station broom being pushed into the appropriate button and the dial set on Black Dog. Needless to say, the Calne railwayman was far from pleased with the Saturday afternoon events at Black Dog when his normal turn of duty was resumed at Calne on the following Monday.

The old station internal telephone also gave the hoaxers plenty of scope to baffle the unsuspecting parcel porter who was on late turn and on his own towards the end of the evening's duty at Calne. From the Calne signal box they would telephone him saying the internal telegram which was about to be dictated was coming from Chippenham. By a smart disguise of voice and by the astute use of some uncommon words in the old G.W.R. book of code (issued in respect of internal telegrams), it was possible to pull off all sorts of hoaxes. The Calne signal box also provided the venue for card playing, the 'school' being made up by the late turn parcel porter, signalman, shunter and booking clerk. If the

Mishap at Calne when train ran into trucks at Calne on the 18.5.1955.
Driver: O. E. Britton; Fireman: D. A. Rogers.

Forming tank special at Calne on the 9.3.1958.

5700 Class on out of gauge load between Calne and Black Dog. These
tanks were going to Ludgershall 10.3.1958.

signalman chanced to have a good hand, then the train from Chippenham was kept waiting at the home signal until it had been played.

The fact that Stanley Bridge Halt was the only intermediate station between Chippenham and Calne listed in the timetable led to some amusing situations when trains arrived at Black Dog in the black-out during the Second World War, particularly if they had Service personnel aboard. Many an unsuspecting Serviceman has unloaded his kit on the platform at Black Dog firmly believing that he had, in fact, reached Calne until either the guard or someone familiar with the line had put him right with an explanation that he had reached a private station which was not in any public timetable.

During the early years of the 1939-45 war, servicemen evacuated from Dunkirk came to R.A.F. Station, Yatesbury, arriving at Calne by special trains. Also from these trains were taken hundreds of pieces of equipment which were stored in every available room until they could be sorted. In the 1914-18 war German prisoners of war used Calne station while travelling to a camp at Yatesbury.

The line had two near misses during German bombing raids in the Second World War. The first was recalled by Mr. Ted Granger, who was parcel porter on duty at Calne on the night that bombs fell in a field alongside the line near Stanley Bridge. He well remembers how the vibration caused by their explosion, was carried by the rails right to the end of the line. Much closer to Calne station were five smaller bombs which fell on part of Harris's private loading platform and store in the early 1940s. The incident, on a dull autumn day, came shortly before the 12.54 p.m. passenger train from Chippenham was due into the platform. The Station Approach road was lined with buses awaiting the Service personnel on the train and in full swing nearby, was the local cattle market. Suddenly, from out of very low cloud, emerged a lone Heinkel 111 whose crew, having come face to face with a literal hive of activity and a loading shed built in an identical manner to an aircraft hangar, could not resist having a go at what for them must have presented a fine target. Unfortunately due to this raid one man was killed and several were injured, but none of them were railwaymen.

AFTER THE WAR

In 1952, with the war long since over, the line was still producing a good revenue. Figures for the year ended September 30th, 1952 showed an income of more than £150,000, while 300,000 incoming and outgoing passengers were dealt with. More than 300,000 consignments comprising 500,000 packages were despatched from Calne by passenger train. On the freight side, about 10,000 wagons containing general goods, livestock, coal, coke and salt were handled, and more than 7,000 weighings were made on the station's 20 ton capacity weighbridge outside the goods office. Upwards of 200 special passenger trains added to the year's traffic figures. At that time three lorries were based at the station for delivery purposes. For several years the branch line's receipts were maintained, but a change came when more and more outgoing traffic from Harris's factory was taken off rail and transferred to the road.

Another severe blow revenuewise came with the closures of R.A.F. Stations Yatesbury and Compton Bassett. The station staff at Calne diminished and by late 1963 freight services had been cut to one each weekday, while the Sunday passenger services had been withdrawn altogether. The line had become one of many in the West Country to be doomed under the Beeching axe. Small consignments of freight were being dealt with at Chippenham and only truck-loads were coming through to Calne.

Early in 1964 came the first intimation that freight services to Calne were to be withdrawn altogether, and also that it was the intention to cease running passenger trains to Calne after June 13th that year. But what British Railways described as 'delays in staff negotiations', resulted in the passenger service being continued after this date.

The last freight train to Calne ran in October 1964. The service should have ended on a Friday, but the only motive power available at Chippenham was a 0—4—0 diesel shunter capable of hauling a maximum of twelve empty wagons. It so happened that in the Calne goods yard were more than a dozen wagons, so the diesel had to make a further trip over the branch on the following day to clear what remained. The diesel shunter arrived in Calne that Saturday hauling two wagons loaded with sleepers (the last firewood for past and present railwaymen ever brought to Calne by train) and a brake van. The sleepers were unloaded by the crew of the train who included guard Mr. Monty Fell. He started his railway career as a lad porter at Calne and later moved to Chippenham. With the wagons offloaded and the others attached to them, all was ready for the return trip to Chippenham. So the last freight service ever to leave Calne did so a day later than originally intended and to the sound of dozens of exploding fog detonators.

In July 1965 the rails were lifted in the Calne goods yard. Just before the withdrawal of the freight service to Calne another historic event took place on the branch line. This came when the Great Western Railway Society ran a steam special from Chippenham to Calne and back. It was the one and only steam passenger train to run to Calne since diesels were introduced on the branch six years previously. Enthusiasts came from far and wide to witness the spectacle. One of them told me he had travelled more than 100 miles 'Just to get a sniff of the inside of the cab of a steam locomotive again.' No-one minded very much that Sunday morning when the train failed to arrive on schedule, but all eyes were turned when the familiar whisp of steam appeared in the distance to signify that the special was passing through Black Dog. The two-coach train arrived in Calne propelled by 0—4—2T No. 1444 which, at that time, was employed on one of the last steam workings in the area—that from Stroud to Chalford. Hundreds of photographs were taken and, for the sole benefit of the photographic enthusiasts, a short run was made from the Calne station platform to a point just past the signal box. After what for everyone must have constituted one of the shortest half-hours ever, the train made its departure.

But few left Calne station until the last steam had passed from view and the final blast on the whistle had been heard. So the last reminder of steam at Calne was lost on that Sunday afternoon in 1964.

THE BIG RUN DOWN

The withdrawal of freight services on the branch was followed by drastic cuts in the staff at Calne. The signal box was closed and quickly became the target of vandals. The station was staffed only until 2 p.m., after which it functioned as an unstaffed halt. Guards issued tickets on the afternoon and evening trains out of Calne and by a telephone installed on the platform they advised the signalman at Chippenham East Box when their trains were ready to leave the terminus. One employee, Mr. Sidney Grainger, who began his railway career at Calne as a goods porter in the 1939-45 war and later became a shunter, remained in sole charge of the station during its last days. With him was a booking clerk, Mrs. Kathleen Williamson, who, like Mr. Grainger, began her duties at Calne during the war years when takings in the booking office alone often exceeded £1,000 in a single day. Mrs. Williamson returned to Calne as a relief clerk to see out the final days of the line.

So the last chapter in more than a century of railway history at Calne was written on September 18th, 1965 when the passenger services were withdrawn. On the previous day the railway authorities honoured Mr. Gordon F. Smith, of Calne, who had travelled regularly on the line for 42 years on his way to and from work at Chippenham, by presenting him with a signalman's lamp. Mr. W. J. Pike, area manager of British Rail at Chippenham, made the presentation and then invited Mr. Smith to have his last ride home by train in the driver's cab. Mr. Smith was one of those who unsuccessfully fought the closure of the line.

D. M.U. standing in Calne platform after the sidings had been lifted.
Photograph Wiltshire Newspapers

THE LAST DAY

On the final day of trains at Calne, groups of railway enthusiasts from all parts of the country were at the station photographing the scene and obtaining last day issue tickets. Hundreds of tickets were issued at the booking office which, although normally closed at 2 p.m., was kept open specially for the occasion. During the day groups of local residents went to the station with the sole object of making sentimental journeys over the branch line. But the climax came with the running of the last ever passenger train. This was the 10.55 p.m. (Saturdays Only) from Chippenham, which, under normal circumstances, would have made the return journey empty. Instead it was scheduled to depart Calne at 11.20 p.m. as a passenger carrying service. More than 140 people waited at Chippenham station for the three-coach suburban diesel unit which was to make the last historic journey to Calne and back.

Driving the train was Mr. Frank Cannon, a railwayman for thirty years, who started at Yeovil and who came to Chippenham in 1939 as a fireman on the steam passenger service to Calne. Mr. Percy Vines, of Calne, the scheduled guard, had to drop out because his son had been married earlier that day, so into the breach stepped Mr. Freddie Bond, who was a passenger shunter at Chippenham before becoming a passenger guard. His duties on the train were shared by the area manager, Mr. W. J. Pike. Passengers aboard included the Mayor and Mayoress of Calne, Councillor and Mrs. Harold Walter Weston.

To the sound of exploding fog detonators and with railway police aboard to ensure that order was kept, the last ever passenger train to Calne with accommodation for 262 passengers slid slowly out of platform four at Chippenham, slightly behind schedule.

Apart from a few impromptu lineside receptions, the journey to Calne passed without incident. No-one boarded the train at Stanley Bridge Halt, but a passenger from Black Dog Halt was the last full-time railwayman to be stationed there, Mr. Douglas Lovelock. More exploding fog detonators heralded the approach of the train to Calne station where at least four hundred people had assembled on the platform. They included Mr. Percy Gleed, who travelled back to Chippenham attired in the Great Western Railway stationmaster's hat he wore while in charge at Calne, and Mr. Tom Moore, goods checker at Calne for 48½ years. Mr. Moore's predecessor in that office, Mr. Tom Cook, was on duty when the first train ran to Calne in 1863. The firing of two signal rockets by the author, who was for some years a member of the railway

Mr. Geoff Taylor sounds the last post for the last train at Calne with driver Frank Cannon in background. 18 September 1965.

Donald Lovelock placing wreath on the last train at Black Dog. 18 September 1965.   *Photographs Wiltshire Newspapers*

clerical staff at Calne, marked the start of the return run.

But before the train moved off the crowd stood in silence as Mr. Geoff Taylor, principal cornet player in Calne Silver Band, sounded 'The Last Post'. A national flag fluttered from the rear of the train as it pulled out of the Calne platform and further down the coaches ticker tape and streamers were released from the windows.

Between Calne and Black Dog Halt 102 fog detonators (one for every year the line had operated) were exploded. In a pall of smoke from the exploding fog detonators, the train pulled into the platform at Black Dog where Mr. Donald Lovelock, who is responsible for many of the photographs in this publication, was waiting to place a wreath on the front buffer beam.

The wreath of laurels was mounted on a board which bore the old Great Western Railway crest in full colour and an inscription which read *In Memoriam. Born 29th October 1863 after giving 101 years of loyal service was killed 18th September 1965.* A black-edged card attached to the wreath had written on it, *In affectionate memory of the Calne railway line 1863-1965. Axed by Beeching, executed by Fraser.*

More exploding fog detonators rattled out like machine gun fire as the train crossed the road bridge at Black Dog. Down the line cars parked at vantage points blew their horns in salute. The diesel's klaxon returned the compliment. At Stanley Bridge Halt a number of people had gathered and, as the train neared Chippenham, the outer home signal, which in its time had held up many trains from Calne, was again set at danger. But the delay was not a long one. The train got underway again, only for it to make an unscheduled stop where the branch line was absorbed into the main line. Someone in the rear coach had pulled the communication cord. Things were quickly put in order and with salvos of fog detonators exploding the train was brought into the platform at Chippenham where more than one hundred people awaited its arrival. Mr. Taylor again sounded 'The Last Post' and Miss Carole Lovelock handed the driver a bouquet of chrysanthemums attached to which was a card with the wording *To the driver of the last ever passenger train from Calne—September 18th, 1965.*

Mr. Cannon was joined at Chippenham station by his wife, the former Miss Joan Smith, daughter of Mr. Tom Smith, who for some years was a steam locomotive driver on the Calne branch line. Before her marriage Mrs. Cannon was for five years during the 1939-45 war, a passenger guard on trains to and from Calne. When the crowds finally dispersed shortly after midnight, the diesel train made its way into the passenger sidings at Chippenham. The final curtain had fallen on the Calne branch line.

THE AFTERMATH

By the following Monday all door nameplates at Calne had been removed, while the station nameboard had also disappeared. But the track remained untouched until shortly after Easter 1967 when a five man team headed by Mr. Ted Bishop, of Bristol, began lifting operations. The work, which lasted until June that year, also entailed the demolition of the station buildings at Black Dog and Stanley Bridge, while lineside wooden huts were burnt. Those engaged on the work found the metal sleepers difficult to remove and the operation had fallen well behind schedule when the Black Bridge, near Chippenham, was reached. Here the lifting operations were brought to an end and for several years that section of the branch line which remained was sometimes used as siding accommodation. Some of the rails which were lifted in 10' lengths found their way to a scrap metal works at Queenborough on the Isle of Sheppey. Metal sleepers and steel chairs were sent to Briton Ferry. Three quarters of a mile of rail at Stanley Bridge Halt was lifted in 60' lengths and relayed on routes still in service. Subsequently the bridge over the A4 at Black Dog was taken out for scrap, the operation being completed without incident at 1.25 a.m. on Sunday, April 21st, 1968.

In 1971 the Black Bridge, near Chippenham, suffered a similar fate, a crane engaged on the operation toppling over in the process without injuring anyone.

At Calne, the station buildings remain—the victims of much vandalism. Calne Town Council owns the site and has earmarked it for industrial development. Stanley Bridge Halt's structure has since become a farm building, while some sections of Black Dog station are in private ownership.

Through the good offices of those who have acquired some of the land which once carried the railway—that section of the track bed from the road bridge at Hazeland to a point not too far from where Stanley Bridge Halt stood—has now become the Marden Nature Trail and offers a picturesque and popular summer walk for the general public.

This has been the story of a branch line which more than justified the faith of those who pioneered its bringing into being. But, like many others, it suffered as a result of being deliberately run down and this constituted a final body blow.

In conclusion, the author would like to express his sincere appreciation of those who have co-operated by supplying information, particularly the former Bowood estate agent, Mr. J. R. Hickish, Mr. R. J. Williams Bulkeley his successor, Wilts. County Council County & Diocesan Archivist, Lord Lansdowne and also local Railwaymen now retired.

Mr. Douglas Lovelock stands on the loading bank at Black Dog after he had demolished the station buildings. *Photo by Wiltshire Newspapers*

CALNE RAILWAY (IMPORTANT DATES)

Location: Chippenham Junction

Act of Incorporation: Calne Railway Act, 15 May 1860

Line worked by G.W.R.: under agreement dated 28th May 1862, by virtue of Section 45 of Act of Incorporation.

Amalgamated with G.W.R.: From 1st July 1892 by Great Western Railway Act, 28th June 1892. S.32.

Date of Opening: 3rd November 1863.

Last Passenger Train: 11.20 p.m. (D.M.U.)
Calne-Chippenham—Saturday, 18 September 1965
Journey details with 142 passengers
Driver: Frank Cannon. *Passenger Guard*: F. Bond.

Freight and Parcels Concentration Scheme, Devizes, Calne, etc. on Chippenham Delivery 2.11.64.

Last Special Troop-Leave Special Train: (12.25) 8 coaches, left Calne 6.15 p.m. 28.5.63.

† *The Bolivers Travels Special* (Last steam hauled train over Calne. Branch, Sunday, Sept. 20, 1964 (Engine No. 1444).

† *Last Booked Time Table Steam Hauled Train* from Calne 1.7 p.m. Calne to Weston S. Mare, Saturday 15.8.64 (Engine No. 82001).

* *Last Booked Freight Train* from Calne 31.10.64 (Saturday) Engine D 2186.

Calne Terminus.

Siphon C Parcels Van Workings Calne
Late 1930s Early 1940s

2.42 p.m.	Paddington	
5.00 p.m.	Manchester	
5.35 p.m.	Portsmouth	
7.05 p.m.	Newcastle	Mondays—Fridays
	Cardiff	
	Paddington	
	Bristol	

Vans berthed in passenger platform after departure of the 9 a.m. service.

Sundays

11.05 a.m.	Paddington
	Manchester
	Newcastle
	Cardiff
	Portsmouth

Vans berthed at 7.30 a.m. by unadvertised passenger service from Chippenham which carried passengers both ways and departed Calne at 7.45 a.m.

On weekdays the Manchester van worked forward by the 5 p.m. Swindon to Bristol service and northwards by the 7.30 p.m. train.

The Portsmouth van was conveyed to Trowbridge by the 5.35 p.m. ex Calne and thence by the 6.38 p.m. from Trowbridge to Portsmouth.

The Newcastle van worked over the Great Central route being attached to the 9.40 p.m. Swindon to York.

1400 Class with tail traffic on the 11.00 a.m. Sundays only Calne/ Chippenham leaving Calne.

APPENDIX I

Reconstruction of Bridge on the Calne Branch

The timber structure near Chippenham which has carried the Calne branch over the River Avon since the opening of that line in 1863 has recently been replaced by a steel bridge satisfying all modern requirements.

The old bridge, which consisted of eight spans of about 22'6" each, was supported at either end on stone abutments, and intermediately on timber piers.

In preparing the design for the new bridge three principal points were kept in view, viz.: (1) A minimum disturbance of the traffic on the branch during reconstruction operations; (2) a minimum amount of temporary work; and (3) facility for inspection and maintenance of the steelwork.

A consideration of the economics of the particular case resulted in the decision to build a two-span bridge, with a brick pier in line with the camp sheathing of the left bank of the river. The width of the new bridge was determined by the scheme of the erection, which involved getting the two main girders into permanent position before removing any vital portions of the old work. In order that this width should not be greater than necessary, a careful survey of the old bridge was made, the plotting of which shewed considerable variation in the width of the timberwork and indicated the extreme points on each side to be cleared when lowering the new girders. The two abutments were remodelled to suit the new steel structure, and, since under the new scheme they would receive loads greater than they were designed for, the foundations were underpinned in order to provide additional security.

The main girders measure 172'10" between the centres of the end bearings, the pier dividing this distance into two spans of 101'8" and 71'2" respectively.

It was decided to design each girder as a continuous braced beam, and in order to reduce the amount of riveting on the ground, to obtain delivery from the builders in two pieces, and to deposit these pieces in place by means of cranes working on the old bridge. An interesting picture of these pieces in transit from Great Bridge to Chippenham was given in the *Magazine* for September last. The heavier of the two weighed 29 tons, was 105'11" in extreme length, and when on trucks stood 13'9½" above rail level. To pick up from trucks and deposit the girderwork in permanent position required the employment of two 36-ton cranes, but calculations shewed that these cranes, when lifting, would unduly stress the old timberwork; therefore certain portions on which the cranes would stand when lifting were temporarily

Photos by British Rail

strengthened by means of auxiliary beams of timber and iron.

The accompanying illustration shews the shorter span of one main girder in position on its bearings and the longer piece being picked up by the cranes preparatory to lowering over the side of the timber structure.

After the two new main girders had been erected, work was begun on the new floor system. During Sunday occupations sections of the old structure were removed and replaced by steel cross-girders and rail-bearers between them, resting directly on the tops of the two main girders. A 4" timber deck was laid over the floor members in order to carry a ballasted cross-sleeper road, and adjacent to lattice steel parapets, footways were formed on each side on a level with the rails.

Strong wind-bracing extends from end to end of the bridge in the plane of the top boom, and transverse bracing at each end and over the pier conveys the effect of the wind down to the bearings. In the plane of the bottom boom horizontal stay-griders are fixed at intervals, these acting also as supports for the inspection gangway which runs the whole length of the bridge. Expansion bearings are provided at each end of the bridge, which is fixed securely to the pier.

The total weight of steel and iron work is about 158 tons. The work was designed by Mr. A. C. Cookson, M.I.C.F., Bridge Assistant to the Chief Engineer. The steel and iron work was supplied by Messrs. The Horseley Bridge and Engineering Co. Ltd., Tipton, Staffs., and the whole of the work at the site was carried out by the Company's men under the supervision of Mr. H. K. Woodward, M.I.C.E., the Divisional Engineer at Bristol.

WORKINGS INTO CALNE, LATE 1930s, EARLY 1940s

Point of origin	Service Arrival Time	Type	Motive Power	Shed	Return Working	
Chippenham	6.10 a.m.	Goods	5700	Chippenham	9.25 a.m.	Pick Up Goods to Chippenham
Chippenham	6.30 a.m.	Passenger	5400 or 4800 (auto)	Chippenham	6.35 a.m.	Passenger to Chippenham
Chippenham	7.15 a.m.	Passenger	5400 or 4800 (auto)	Chippenham	7.25 a.m.	Passenger worked through to Box
Chippenham	8.20 a.m.	Mixed	5700	Chippenham	8.25 a.m.	Passenger (at one time the engine worked back on the 9 a.m.
Box	8.55 a.m.	Passenger	5400 or 4800 (auto)	Chippenham	9.00 a.m.	Passenger Became 10.20 a.m. Chippenham—Worthing
Bristol	10.38 a.m.	Passenger	4500 (B Set)	Bristol Bath Road	10.50 a.m.	Passenger worked to Bath (via Box) and Bristol
Chippenham	11.25 a.m.	Goods	5700	Chippenham	1.25 p.m.	Goods to Chippenham
Westbury	12.08 p.m.	Passenger	5400 (auto)	Westbury	12.20 p.m.	Passenger to Chippenham
Chippenham	1.07 p.m.	Passenger	5400 (auto)	Westbury	1.12 p.m.	Passenger Became 1.50 p.m. Chippenham to Westbury
Bristol	2.06 p.m.	Passenger	4500 (B Set)	Bristol Bath Road	2.42 p.m.	Passenger worked to Bath (via Box) and Bristol
Chippenham	2.35 p.m.	Goods	5700	Chippenham	5.55 p.m.	Goods to Chippenham
Westbury	4.45 p.m.	Passenger	5400 (auto)	Westbury	5.00 p.m.	Passenger to Chippenham
Chippenham	5.32 p.m.	Passenger	5400 (auto)	Westbury	5.35 p.m.	Passenger Became 5.50 p.m. Chippenham to Westbury
Chippenham	6.50 p.m.	Passenger	4800, 5400, 5700	Chippenham	7.05 p.m.	Passenger to Chippenham
Chippenham	8.45 p.m.	Passenger	4800 or 5400 (auto)	Chippenham	9.00 p.m.	Passenger to Chippenham
Chippenham	9.55 p.m.	Passenger	4800 or 5400 (auto)	Chippenham	10.05 p.m.	Passenger to Chippenham
Chippenham	11.05 p.m. (Weds. & Sats only)	Passenger	4800 or 5400 (auto)	Chippenham	11.10 p.m.	Passenger to Chippenham
				Saturdays Only		
Swindon	12.50 p.m.		4500	Swindon	1.05 p.m.	Passenger to Weston-Super-Mare
Bristol	3.05 p.m.		4500	Bristol Bath Road	3.15 p.m.	Passenger to Bath & Bristol
				Sundays Only		
Chippenham	7.30 a.m.	Passenger (not in public timetable)	5400 or 4800 (auto)	Chippenham	7.45 a.m.	Passenger Became 8.10 a.m. to Swindon
Swindon	10.30 a.m.	Passenger	5400 or 4800 (auto)	Chippenham	11.05 a.m.	Passenger to Chippenham
Chippenham	5.05 p.m.	Passenger	5400 or 4800 (auto)	Chippenham	5.25 p.m.	Passenger to Chippenham
Chippenham	Evening trains	Passenger	5400 or 4800 (auto)	Chippenham		
Bristol	9.40 p.m.	Passenger	4500	Bristol Bath Road	9.50 p.m.	Passenger to Chippenham
Chippenham	10.35 p.m.	Passenger	5400 or 4800 (auto)	Chippenham	10.40 p.m.	Passenger to Chippenham

13th. June 1930

Note of interview with Mr. Pole, Divisional Superintendent, Great Western Railway.

Mr. Pole stated that Cockram is receiving £4 per week & an additional 5% from the Great Western Railway to cover any overtime he does outside the usual hours.

The takings at Black Dog Station amount roughly to about £2000 a year, and, therefore, this would not be sufficient to appoint another Stationmaster of the same grade as Cockram, and the proposal is to appoint a first grade Porter (a married man); he would get from 48/- to 50/- a week and would be quite capable of doing all the duties at Black Dog Siding.

Mr. Pole stated that if Lord Lansdowne terminated the present agreement he hoped that Cockram's cottage would be available for the new man.

It was arranged that Mr. Pole should communicate the result of his interview with Capt. Hood to the official at Paddington, and Capt. Hood promised to let Lord Lansdowne know the Company's proposal.

Two interesting letters.

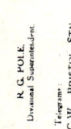

GREAT WESTERN RAILWAY.

R.G. POLE, Divisional Superintendent.

Telegram:
DIVISIONAL G.W. BRISTOL STN.

Telephone:
9400 (PRIVATE BRANCH EXCHANGE)

Your Reference —

DIVISIONAL SUPERINTENDENT'S OFFICE,
TEMPLE MEADS STATION,
BRISTOL.

Please quote this reference —
A1/116.

12th July, 1930

Dear Sir,

With reference to my interview with you on June 13th, I have submitted the Marquis of Lansdowne's views to my Headquarters at Paddington, and am pleased to inform you that it has been agreed and the Chief Accountant instructed that the Agreement made between the Marquis of Lansdown and the Great Western Railway Company in 1875 shall be terminated as from the commencement of the current half-year, i.e. 1st July 1930.

With regard to the remarks that passed in reference to Mr. Cockram's successor and the house at Black Dog Station, I have to inform you that the man chosen to succeed Mr. Cockram is Porter Lovelock, who is 29 years of age and has been with the Company 10 years, and who, I think, you will find will be most courteous and obliging and do all he can to co-operate with you in every way in connection with your railway business.

In the circumstances I shall be glad to hear that you can allow him to have the house which has been vacated by Mr. Cockram.

Do you wish the arrangements in connection with the telephones to continue, please?

Yours faithfully,

Captain A.O. Hood,
Bowood Estate Office,
CALNE.

CALNE BRANCH —— Passengers change at Chippenham.

TRAINS FROM CALNE.

Fares.			Starting from	Week Days.								
1st class.	2nd class.	3rd class.		Ex. 1 & 2 class.	1 & 2 class.	a.m.	Ex. 1 & 2 class.	a.m.	1, 2, 3 class.	p.m.	1 & 2 class.	1 & 2 class.
1/6	1/0	0/5¼	**Calne** . . dep.	8 30	8 45	...	9 45	10 45	1 35	4 25	6 50	...
			Chippenham arr.	8 45	9 35	11 0	11	11 0	1 50	4 40	7 10	...
5/11	4/0	2/6	Chippenham dep.	...	9 45	11 42	12 40	2 0	4 53	8	...	
			Bristol . arr.	...	10 40	12 25	2 0	2 50	5 40	9 5	...	
14/8	10/11	6/8½	Chippenham dep.	...	11 45	2 10	2 10	...	7 25	...		
9/0	6/3	3/10	Weymouth arr.	...	2 30	5 20	...	10 5	9 20	...		
			Salisbury arr.	...	1 35	4 5	4 5	...	...	...		
18/0	13/5	8/3½	Chippenham dep. 8 55	11 12	1 0	3 42	5 25	8 33	...			
			Padding arr. 11 15	2 40	5 45	6 10	9 0	11 5	...			

TRAINS TO CALNE.

Fares.			Starting from	DISTANCE FROM CALNE.	Week Days.								
1st class.	2nd class.	3rd class.			Ex. 1 & 2 class.	1 & 2 class.	a.m.	Ex. 1, 2, 3 class.	a.m.	p.m.	Ex. 1 & 2 class.	1 & 2 class.	Ex. 1 & 2 class.
18/0	13/5	8/3½	**Padding** dep.	99¾	...	6 0	7 5	9 15	...	11 45	2 0	4 50
1/6	1/0	0/5¼	Chippenham arr.	5½	...	9 45	12 35	11 40	...	1 55	4 50	7 15
9/0	6/3	3/10	Salisbury dep.	46	6 50	...	10 25	...	1 40	...	6 25	
14/8	10/11	6/8½	Weymouth dep.	80¼	6 50	...	9 0	...	12 50	...	5 20	
			Chippenham arr.		8 45	...	12 30	...	3 33	...	8 25	
5/11	4/0	2/6	Bristol . dep.	30¼	8 10	...	11 30	12 15	...	2 55	4 30	7 45
			Chippenham arr.		8 53	...	12 40	12 53	...	3 38	5 20	8 30
		2/6	Chippenham dep.	...	9 0	9 50	1 0	...	3 45	5 25	8 35
		...	**Calne** .. arr.	...	9 15	10 5	1 15	...	4 0	5 40	8 50

For Intermediate Stations between Bath and Bristol, Chippenham and London, Westbury and Salisbury, and Westbury and Weymouth, see pages 36 and 37.

Part of a G.W.R. timetable of 1865.

Chippenham and Calne

	CHIPPENHAM	STANLEY BRIDGE HALT	BLACK DOG HALT	CALNE
	d			a

CHIPPENHAM	6 05	8 07	8 53	9 55	11 55	13 40	14 55	15 36	16 31	17 12	17 56	18 37	19 33	21 12	22 55
STANLEY BRIDGE HALT	6 11	8 13		10 01	12 01	13 46			16 37	17 18		18 43	19 39		23 01
BLACK DOG HALT															
CALNE	6 20	8 22	9 06	10 10	12 10	13 55	15 08	15 49	16 46	17 27	18 09	18 52	19 48	21 25	23 10

Calne and Chippenham

CALNE	7 05	8 26	9 15	11 10	13 10	14 05	15 11	16 02	16 50	17 32	18 17	19 05	19 55	21 35
BLACK DOG HALT		8 29						†	†		†		†	†
STANLEY BRIDGE HALT	7 14	8 36	9 24	11 19	13 19	14 14			16 59			19 14	20 04	
CHIPPENHAM	7 20	8 41	9 30	11 25	13 25	14 20	15 23	16 15	17 05	17 45	18 30	19 20	20 10	21 48

Heavy figures indicate through carriages
For general notes see page 3

† Calls when required to set down and take up passengers. Those wishing to alight must inform the Guard at Chippenham or Calne, and passengers desiring to join should give the necessary hand signal to the driver. Trains depart from Black Dog Halt 3 minutes after leaving Stanley Bridge Halt and 3 minutes after leaving Calne. Trains not shown to call at Stanley Bridge Halt depart from Black Dog Halt 9 minutes after leaving Chippenham.

British Railways 4 January to 13 June 1965 timetable

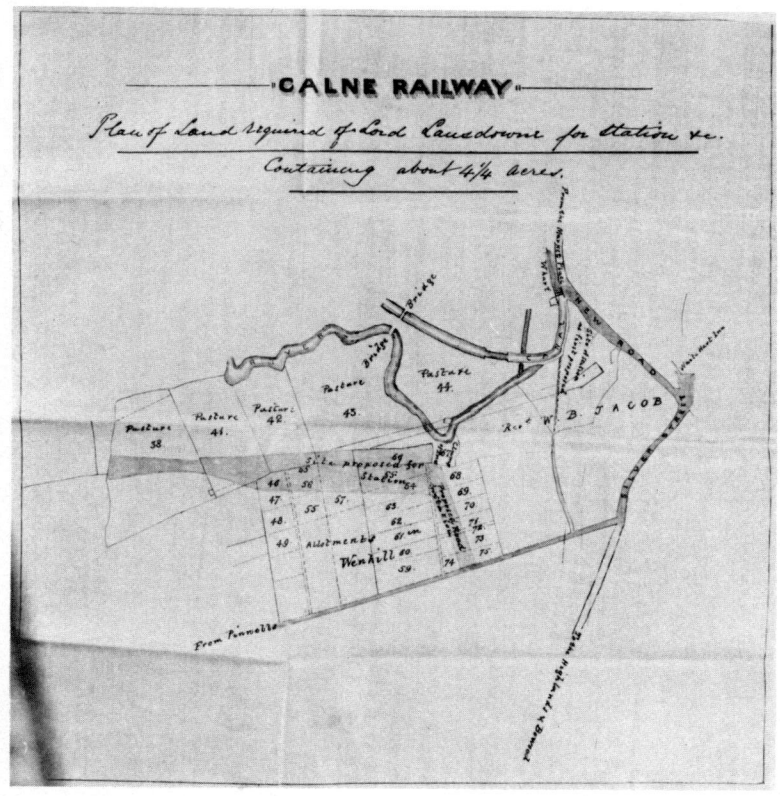

One of the original plans for Calne station.

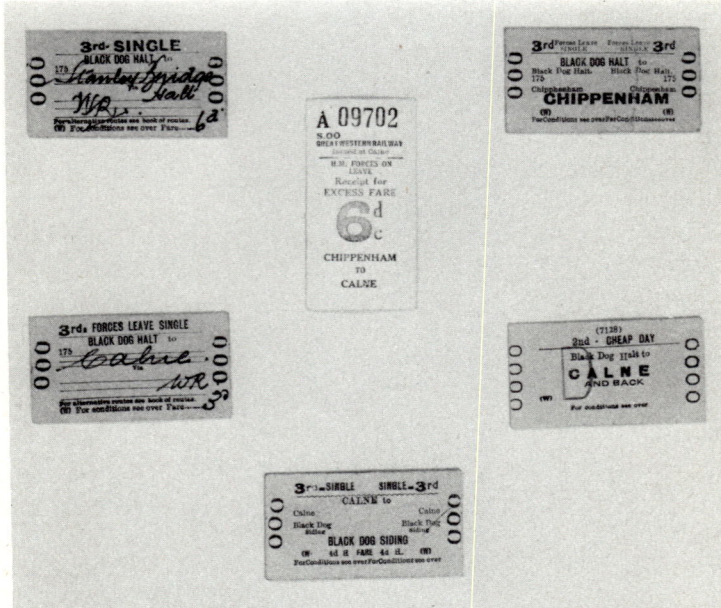

Calne Railway share certificate.

Selection of tickets.